YOUR STORY IS NOT DONE

YOUR STORY IS NOT DONE

JORGE & KAT VAZQUEZ

Contents

Introduction

There is no such thing as coincidence—like this book. You were meant to be reading these words right now. You're looking for answers anywhere and everywhere because you have felt shipwrecked and forgotten, broken and battered. Your sails are ripped and flapping in the wind, your world has capsized. The raging storms and bitter winds have stolen your passion and silenced your voice.

Scattered. Scared. Fear swallowing you up.

And sorrow has been guiding you. You find yourself surging closer and closer to the rocks. Your dreams are crushed by the surge because your hope has been slammed against the boulders and shattered into pieces. Your heart is crying out, but your lips can't even conjure a word. Your soul is sick with bitterness.

But your heavenly Father heard your lament—your ode to hope lost and faith fading. *Did you hear His reply?*

You've only known one part of the story. Your life has endured much heart break. You've experienced the pressing—but not yet the Promise. He is saying, "Your Story Is Not Done"....

As the title proclaims, the purpose of this book is to convince you and everyone around you that indeed _your story is not done!_

You may be facing the fight of your life as you read these words. Perhaps you are in a weary season of recovery from battle after battle. All you feel is defeated and lost. Or maybe you've experienced several victories in seasons past, but now it feels like the best is just a distant memory. Regardless of what season in life you may be navigating, I stand here to deliver a simple truth to you: the Author and Finisher of the universe, the One who spoke life into existence, is wanting and willing to take over the story of your life.

He is wanting to rewrite the mistakes of your past. He is waiting to cross out the storylines that have held you back. He is here to restore you to your proper standing _in Him_. He is turning the page of your story!

He will fill your sails again, taking you from the dormant places and guiding you back into the flow of His presence. You will feel alive again! You will feel free again—stirred with fresh hope to fulfill your purposes.

There is only One who can rewrite the script of our life. His name is Jesus...and when He takes over your life, _Your Story Is Not Done!_

Stories

We as humans are constantly on a search for our storyline. Perceptions and paradigms are the stories we tell about our lives. As human beings we are always looking for meaning in our experiences, and tying those meanings together in a narrative that makes sense to us. Each one of us are driven to look for meaning: The meaning of us in our lives, families, communities, nation and world. We are looking for identity.

The truth is that the only person who can tell us with final authority who we really are is our Creator, God. And the only one who can rewrite our story is Jesus Christ, the Author of our faith.

God's Story

God the Father is God the author. He is the originator of all that exists. It existed first in His mind that everything took shape.

God the Son—Jesus our Rescuer—is God the Artisan. As the Artist and Creator of all that exists, He brought into being all that originally was designed in His Father's mind. But not only that, He continually holds everything together. He constantly intercedes for us, and is creatively working things out for our benefit.

God the Holy Spirit is God the agent who reveals these facts to both our mind and spiritual understanding. Then they become both real and relative to us.

To explain how your reality—your story—collides with God's story, we need to go back to an ancient book that is the most remarkable book in history. This book has impacted societies and empires, telling the most beautiful Love Story.

The Bible, against what most think, isn't a book of rules or a book of legends. The Bible is a true story. It's a daring rescue story about a Hero who travels a very long way to win back his lost prize. It's a love story about a brave prince who leaves his palace, his kingdom—everything—to rescue the one He loves. Its the most wonderful of tales!

The best part about this story is that it's true! There are lots of stories in the Bible, but all the stories are telling one main story—the story of how God loves His children and comes to rescue them.

Sometimes we all feel like we need to be rescued. Maybe you're searching for that lifeline right now. Maybe you're feeling like you're drowning.

You're overwhelmed with fear, or your heart feels dry, you're burned out, and you're just not so sure you believe in this "all loving" God like you thought you did at one time. You feel forgotten, lost, left, abandoned. Maybe you're saying "God doesn't love me." Your life looks more like a nightmare. You feel like fear is stalking you. You wear it. It's familiar, pulling it on like a coat weighing heavy across your shoulders.

Life has happened to you. In any other story, it would all be over, finished and it would have been…. The End.

But not in this Story.

God loves his children, He loves you too much to let the story end there.

Even though he knew he would suffer, God had a plan— an awesome plan! You see, in spite of everything, God doesn't stop chasing us down with his love. His love is perfect. It's the stuff that redeems and rewrites stories—because He loves us with an unbreakable, unmovable, for always and forevermore love. He is incapable of leaving you and has *already* written your comeback story.

[1]

Why Your Story?

Why me? Have you ever found yourself asking that question?

I know I have. Usually that inner monologue is triggered after something bad happens or goes wrong that we can't explain. Like a woolen, yarn ball unraveling, our thoughts start to take a tumble. "Why me" normally leads next to the famous complaint: "Why now?" The yarn ball of thoughts start to spiral downward still, tumbling and tumbling, getting more and more personal, and then finally crashes face first into the very personal and cold concrete of: "Why does this always happen to me?"

These questions are part of a natural thought process to every person on the face of the earth. It is common to feel that bad things only happen to you— especially in the moments after something tragic. When things go wrong it's easy to just feel that only bad things happen to you and "Why me" comes stumbling out of your mouth

I want you for a second to flip that notion and ask yourself "why me" again, but this time we're going to do a little experiment. We are going to put a new film in the projector so to speak.

So ponder this: Why would the Author who hung the stars in the sky want to take over my story? Why my story? Why would God care enough to change the outcome of my story? Why would He bother? With the frame of reference changed from your perspective and paradigms to your Creator's, the one who has good plans and a future in store for you, is not intimidated by time (your age), or where you are right now. So with that film loaded into the projector, let's proceed with the experiment...

Why not? Why not you? Why not your story?

> **Ephesians 1:4-5 spells it out: "For he chose us in him before the creation of the world...In love he predestined us for adoption to sonship through Jesus Christ, in accordance with his pleasure and will..."**

I want you to know that Jesus had you in mind when he took on the ultimate sacrifice. Rewriting your story was His mission, and you are His prize!

You're probably thinking ...yeah right! There is no way Jesus had me in mind. There is no way that He would want to turn my life around. This may be something hard for you to believe, but the fact is that Jesus sacrificed everything to seek you out. In fact His mission was not just for you but everyone.

2 Peter 3:8-10 shows:

> **"But do not forget this one thing, dear friends: With the Lord a day is like a**

thousand years, and a thousand years are like a day. The Lord is not slow in keeping his promise, as some understand slowness. Instead he is patient with you, not wanting anyone to perish, but everyone to come to repentance."

Jesus doesn't want anyone to perish. The issue that stands in the way is us. It is up to us to embrace His gift. We have to acknowledge Him by accepting Him as our Lord and Savior. We must allow Him to bring the rewrite. We have to allow His hand to move upon our lives in surrender with humility. In our yield, He begins the process of rewriting our story.

I remember when I wrote my first book "No More Rejection." I was done with the manuscript and it had been edited four times. I was at the stage where I was seeking endorsements from prominent preachers and people to help promote the book.

I was literally days from sending it off for publishing when a dear friend who was endorsing the book called and asked to help edit. My first thought was, "Man, this thing has been edited four times! It's ready to go! It doesn't need anymore editing." My friend insisted that it may need a bit of tweaking, perhaps a rewrite here or there.

"Rewrites?" I thought. "What? My book doesn't need any rewrites!" My wife and I were ordained evangelists, speakers, we knew the Word. And on top of that, I had been researching and working on this book for a few years now. It was like my baby! I thought surely this book is solid, "good to go." My pride and impatience were impeding a very much needed rewrite—there were some things I just didn't see. And thank goodness for my friend's experience as an established minister and author, because he made suggestions making it better, for greater impact!

Here's the backstory, you see my friend was a very established theologian who not only added "street-cred" with the Christian academic crowd, his insight into the Greek language allowed me to have the perfect ending to my book. His knowledge allowed the perfect rewrite of my final chapter that drove home an emphatic point about God's love for us.

Without his experience and touch, the book would have missed the mark I was wanting to hit. I thank God for my friend wanting to intervene to help me with a special rewrite. In the end it was up to me to humble myself and allow him to do so. I had to submit what I was in control over and have someone else who was better equipped to take over. Humility to surrender made all the difference with the outcome!

Just like my friend's background and expertise allowed me to have a great rewrite for my book, Jesus is looking to take over your life and rewrite your story. If only you would let Him take control to help. Trust me, He knows what He is doing!

Jesus in fact has the perfect background, one that laid the foundations of this earth and the universe. The Bible explains that Jesus is the "Alpha and Omega"—the beginning and the end. **"I am the Alpha and the Omega," says the Lord God, "who is, and who was, and who is to come, the Almighty." Revelation 1:8**

Jesus is the beginning, the end, and everything in between. His power is beyond comprehension or calculation.

It goes on to say in **Hebrews 12:2 (KJV) "Looking unto Jesus the author and finisher of our faith; who for the joy that was set before him endured the cross, despising the shame, and is set down at the right hand of the throne of God."**

I am pretty sure that experience qualifies Jesus to rewrite your story. Don't you think? Not only is He the beginning and the end or "Alpha and Omega", He is also the "Author and Finisher of our faith." When we place our trust/faith in Him, Jesus takes over and authors our faith. He perfects it just like a jeweler polishing a priceless jewel. The Lord will perfect our story by authoring and finishing it for His glory. We see how Jesus works in Romans when Paul, one of the Apostles writes:

> **"And we know that in all things God works for the good of those who love him, who have been called according to his purpose. For those God foreknew he also predestined to be conformed to the image of his Son, that he might be the firstborn" among many brothers and sisters. And those he predestined, he also called; those he called, he also justified; those he justified, he also glorified." Romans 8:28-30**

Jesus is all-knowing. He sees and knows everything. Not even time or space can hold back His plans for you! The Bible says He goes before you to "work" all things for your good. He is directing and even redirecting all things to ensure you are positioned for His purposes that bring God glory. He will bring people, arrange circumstances and align situations "just so" in order for you to be at just the right place and right time to be caught up in His ways! The key is placing your trust in Him.

I know that placing your trust in someone is not an easy thing. Especially when the people in your life ended up dropping the ball, disappointing, or even abandoning you.

People will disappoint you from time to time—but Jesus never will. In fact He is incapable of leaving you.

I want to prove to you that Jesus will never disappoint you, and that He is more than deserving to hold your trust. Look at the next verse in Hebrews 12. In verse 3 it goes on to say:

> **"Consider him who endured such opposition from sinners, so that you will not grow weary and lose heart."**
> **Hebrews 12:3**

The Author of the book of Hebrews, after explaining how Jesus was the Author and Perfecter of our faith, goes on to lay the case—revealing Jesus' real motive for laying down His life.

Jesus endured "opposition from sinners," which actually was a nice way of saying He was bruised, battered and then killed, setting a bar of how much He wanted your heart's freedom. Now that is love!

He was brutally tortured and sacrificed on a Roman cross over two thousand years ago for you to have the incredible opportunity of salvation. His sacrifice was paramount, making anything we could ever go through pale in comparison. Christ being the ultimate example of trusting God through death, hell, and the grave—Paul made sure to point that out, rallying his audience that if Jesus did what He did, we certainly don't have to "grow weary and lose heart."

If this type of sacrifice and compassion is not a sign of someone worthy of your trust, I don't know what is! Trust Him with your story. He had you in mind. He knew you would be weary in this season you're in. He knew you would be tempted to lose heart. Your story was on His heart as He contemplated the pain of The Cross, and He endured to win your freedom and gain the chance to rewrite your story!

So what would it look like if you placed your total trust in Jesus? What would His rewrite for your story look like? We see in Jeremiah what His plans are for you:

**"For I know the plans I have for you,"
declares the Lord, "plans to prosper
you and not to harm you, plans to give
you hope and a future." Jeremiah 29:11**

Jesus' plans for you are simple. He is planning to prosper you, not harm you as some people have falsely portrayed God to be. He plans to give you something that is very rare these days, something that is beyond priceless: Hope! His hope will fill you with life, freedom, purpose and a future!

Many of you know that I am bi-vocational. I have the privilege of serving both in the church world and in the corporate arena. A few years ago I took over an Inside Sales office with over 100 employees. It was a big move literally as it moved us from Kentucky to Florida. We felt God's hand all over this opportunity to serve. Even though it was a major sacrifice to transplant our family and move thousands of miles away from family, we knew God was calling us to do so.

The corporate job I took was a mission requiring a complete turnaround when I stepped into position. The office had been suffering 125% attrition and the environment was toxic. You could feel the uneasiness in the air. When I began to pray and assess the situation I realized that the team lacked one major ingredient for success. It lacked hope. It was as if the team had given up on their future.

I began having daily huddles with the entire team of over 100 employees.

The huddles were big pep talks that were meant to help them build hope. Hope in themselves, in their job and in their family, in their future. After being prompted by a team member that asked "how are you so positive and hopeful?" I explained I have an endless supply of hope and I am always willing to share. You see as a believer in Jesus we have an endless supply of hope and our mission is to demonstrate that to a world that is lost and hopeless. The more the team got to know me day in and day out they quickly realized that my endless source of hope came from my faith in Jesus. I never had to preach it, I just simply lived it and that gave them a reason to ask, "Where do you get that?" Is it easy to stay hopeful? No, it is a constant battle against this world that loves to promote victimhood and bad news, fear and greed. The key is to continually remind myself who is driving my life, while constantly trusting Him everyday with the details.

Trust is such a hard thing to extend. It is almost universal to roll one's eyes when you hear someone say, "Trust me." Trust is something that we keep behind the guarded walls of our heart. It is the hardest thing to extend as it involves becoming vulnerable and relying on someone else to not disappoint you.

Today with the advent of technology and news feeds, we see so much bad news, corruption and deception on a daily basis. It has made it almost impossible to trust what you hear and that is effecting our perceptions. Technology has evolved to the point where videos can be created that can show famous people saying things they did not say… completely fabricated and used as a phishing scheme all to get more clicks on a link! Truth is under fire and makes it even harder to trust. As fake, social media ad's pop up, it makes it hard to even believe what you see these days, so how much harder is it to trust God… who you can't?

Yet Jesus is not just trustworthy, He is perfect and His will for us is worth the effort and vulnerability. In this age we live in it is more important to cast our trust on Him. One of my favorite verses is found in Proverbs 3.

"Trust in the Lord with all your heart and lean not on your own understanding; in all your ways submit to him, and he will make your paths straight." Proverbs 3:5-6

As this world becomes harder and harder to understand— let alone navigate the confusing waters—we must fully trust and rely on God with all our heart.

As a boy I played competitive baseball. My mom would always remind me to make sure that I would play with my "heart and soul." That was her one ask if I was going to give of my time that it would be with everything I had inside of me.

That is exactly what Father God wants us to do. Give Him your heart and in return He will "make your paths straight." Meaning He will not just guide you but actually make the way you are going straight and right on target.

I had a baseball coach that would always preach to us "don't let the highs get too high, and the lows get too low, keep straight and level so you get there faster!"

The point being the straighter the route you're taking the faster you will achieve your goal. That's exactly what God wants for your life. He want to make your path straight so you accomplish His plan for your life. A deep, heart-rooted trust in Jesus is needed to unlock His plan being manifested in your life.

I want to prove to you that He is worthy of your trust. And He really is for you, working things out for your good.

He is a legitimately good Father. In our society today that's nearly impossible to understand. After all, we have been labeled "the fatherless generation." Even if you have no radar for what that looks and feels like, I want to prove how true and real it is from a simple angle.

We belong to Him simply because He deliberately chose to create us as the object of His own affection. And just how much did He love us? He bought us again at the incredible price of his own, laid-down life and shed blood.

We are His birthright, His sons and daughters by relation, and we are His inheritance. Loaded, right? We belong to Him by virtue of the fact that His own body was laid down with *this* day in mind. There is an intimate identity involved: We are in truth a part of Him and He is a part of us. We are exceedingly precious to Him. But just like sheep we are prone to wander...to be influenced by our fears and timidity, our stubbornness and stupidity, our perverse habits are all swaying and luring our minds and affections away from Whom we belong to: The Good Father, our trustworthy guide and loving caregiver. And yet despite our human condition and characteristics, Jesus chooses us, bought us with the greatest price, calls us by name, makes us His own and delights in caring for us. He literally lays Himself out for us continually. He is ever guiding us by His Spirit, He is ever working on our behalf to make sure we benefit from His care. His love never gives up, never stops. It's forever active, unbreakable, and always exceedingly for us.

Do you want to meet Him?

[2]

Meet the Author

If you haven't met Him yet, I want to introduce you to The Author.

Jesus is the Author and Finisher of life itself. He is the One who literally hung the moon and stars in the sky. Christians have the priceless privilege of looking to Jesus as our leader. Something cool to point out, the Greek word translated "author" is the same one translated "Captain" in Hebrews 2:10, referring to Him the Captain of our salvation, the One who guides us, pioneers and leads us through the uncharted waters of life's stormy seas. Jesus specializes in both creation and restoration, and if you let him He will create a master work in your life.

Today we see so many descriptions of Jesus. Some describe Him as a teacher, or as a prophet. Some feel He was just a historical figure. Countless people have received Him as their one and true Savior.

So who is Jesus really? When I get asked that in discussions about Jesus I always point to John Chapter one:

"In the beginning was the Word, and the Word was with God, and the Word was God. He was with God in the beginning. Through him all things were made; without him nothing was made that has been made. In him was life, and that life was the light of all mankind. The light shines in the darkness, and the darkness has not overcome it." John 1:1-5

John 1 is a a loaded chapter that goes into detail of who Jesus really is. First and foremost, He is God Almighty. The scripture shows how Jesus was there in the beginning of life with God and yet was also God. This is a fact that many people do not realize: Jesus is not just the Son of God but that He is also God. I believe this is something that we all have to stop and recognize daily. In fact when ever I sign one of my books I tend to write this simple yet powerful reminder: "God is good....and Jesus is God!." This simple phrase hits at the heart of the two biggest misconceptions about God. It points out how God is good—not an angry revengeful God—and that Jesus is also God. Let's stop and ponder this notion for a minute.

Jesus is not just the Son of God. He is not just our personal Savior. He is part of the Trinity. You see God is three in one. He is God the Father, God the Son (Jesus), and God the Holy Spirit. If we examine this we can see the parallel in ourselves. The Bible explains that we were "made in His image." We are also comprised of a mind, body and spirit. Think about it. When you are reasoning you are using your mind. When you are acting on your thoughts you are using your body. Lastly when you have that sense of feeling (not just the 5 sense kind) it is your spirit. Likewise God the Father moves in similar fashion. The dynamic among the Trinity that boggles my mind is where one ends and the other begins. This leads me to the next big description of Jesus in John chapter 1: Jesus is the Word.

The original Greek word used here is Logos. Logos is defined in Webster's dictionary as:

> "the divine wisdom manifest in the creation,
> government, and redemption of the world
> and often identified with the second person
> of the Trinity."

Jesus' divinity was used to manifest all of creation. He literally gave and keeps giving life! In fact John goes on to explain how, "through him all things were made; without him nothing was made that has been made."

Just think about that. Everything that has ever been made was made through Him. That means that you, your family, your friends, your whole world was made through Jesus! In Hebrews the Bible reiterates this point.

"By faith we understand that the universe was formed at God's command, so that what is seen was not made out of what was visible." Hebrews 11:3

Jesus formed the whole universe. He is the master Creator and master Author. Wow! Just take a moment to let that sink in...marvel at that fact! The vast, endless universe we can't even comprehend was all created at God's command by Jesus! He is all powerful, He is all knowing, and He wants to create your story. The book of Hebrews in the New

Testament also explains in an earlier chapter that Jesus not only created it all, but it is He who also sustains everything.

"The Son is the radiance of God's glory and the exact representation of his being, sustaining all things by his powerful word." Hebrews 1:3

Jesus holds all of us together. Science has shown that atoms and molecules are held together by energy. I am here to tell you that Jesus is the one that commands that energy to bind together. Without Jesus everything that you see, know, or even imagine would fall apart. These two notions of Jesus both as the Creator of everything and the One who holds everything together, is so important that it was brought up over and over in scripture to reinforce the point!

In Colossians 1 Paul writes:

"The Son is the image of the invisible God, the firstborn over all creation. For in him all things were created: things in heaven and on earth, visible and invisible, whether thrones or powers or rulers or authorities; all things have been created through him and for him. He is before all things, and in him all things hold together. And he is the head of the body, the church; he is the beginning and the firstborn from among the dead, so that in everything he might have the supremacy. For God was pleased to have all his fullness dwell in him, and through him to reconcile to himself all things, whether

things on earth or things in heaven, by making peace through his blood, shed on the cross." Colossians 1:15- 20

Again the picture is painted that Jesus not only created all, what is seen and unseen, but that He indeed holds everything together. How is He not the right person for you to trust with your story?

This verse is also used to explain that it was Jesus who was used by God to make peace with mankind. This is the most important part of who Jesus is in regard to our story. Jesus is our Savior. You see, ever since people gave in to sin at the fall of man, sin was introduced to mankind. This has kept us from having real fellowship with God. The ultimate consequence of sin is separation from God.

The way to best explain it is see Jesus as an eternal filter (so to speak) that allows our imperfection to be removed in order for us to be able to come into God's presence and Kingdom. You see God is perfect and therefore by definition that which is perfect can not connect with something that is imperfect. Let's use the filter analogy. If God is like pure water, it can not come into contact with contaminated water without first filtering out the impurities to make that water pure. That is where Jesus comes in. God cared so much for us that He wanted to make a way for us to come to Him. In fact Jesus himself points this out in John Chapter 14:

"Jesus answered, "I am the way and the truth and the life. No one comes to the Father except through me." John 14:6

Jesus is the only way to be reconciled and returned to God the Father. His death on the cross led to our being purified by His precious, perfect blood. As a result, we now

27

have a way into the Father's Kingdom—thus rewriting and restoring our story!

Now, I want you to think about what Jesus did on that cross. He did not just die for us. He took on our shame, our guilt and our sin. Imagine for a second the most shameful thing you have ever done. The thing that perhaps no one knows, but it replays in the back of your mind as something that is unforgivable. Now just imagine the weight of that shame and begin to multiply that times the same one shameful event for every person that has and will walk the face of this earth. You see, *all* that was on Jesus on that cross. Not only one shameful sin but each and every sin of every human throughout all mankind—past, present and future. He took on the unimaginable weight of all that guilt and shame just to make the way for us. As if that wasn't hard enough, the worse part was that at that very moment that all of that sin was placed on Him, He suffered the most painful thing ever: God the Father turned His back on His son. Jesus was separated from his Father in that moment. He was isolated and alone carrying the ultimate load, multiplied by every human that ever walked on earth. We see this in the Gospel of Mathew:

> **"From noon until three in the afternoon darkness came over all the land. About three in the afternoon Jesus cried out in a loud voice, *"Eli, Eli, lema sabachthani?"* (which means "My God, my God, why have you forsaken me?")." Matthew 27:45-46**

Jesus cared enough to rewrite your story when he became even the most vile, sinful being at the price of being separated from His perfect loving Father. The good news is that Jesus conquered sin and the grave as He rose from the dead three days after taking on our sin on the cross. It was God's plan all along from the beginning of time. In fact the book Colossians goes on to state:

> **"Once you were alienated from God and were enemies in your minds because of your evil behavior. But now he has reconciled you by Christ's physical body through death to present you holy in his sight, without blemish and free from accusation— if you continue in your faith, established and firm, and do not move from the hope held out in the gospel. This is the gospel that you heard and that has been proclaimed to every creature under heaven, and of which I, Paul, have become a servant. Colossians 1:15-23**

Now we see that Jesus sacrifice has made us without blemish in God's sight. Making us pure and reestablishing our relationship to God the Father.

I want to point out another facet of who Jesus is. In John one it also describes Jesus as "life" and "light":

> **"In him was life, and that life was the light of all mankind. The light shines in the darkness, and the darkness has not overcome it." John 1:4-5**

Jesus is "the Light" and no matter what darkness you are facing He will overcome it for you. All you have to do is trust Him, trust Him with your story. He is here to give you real life. You see the enemy of our soul tries to deceive us into thinking that life is found in the darkness yet in reality there is no life there at all.

Jesus is true life and He wants to extend that to us. Jesus wants to light up your life! He is **"The true light that gives light to everyone." John 1:9**

Stop hiding in the darkness one minute longer. Let Him eclipse and shatter the shame, the lies you've been believing and living under for so long, keeping you imprisoned. That's not who you are! The true story of Christ's body willingly laid down on Calvary's Cross was all for *this* day in mind: for you!

The most important decision you will ever make is when you know your heart is colliding with the presence of Jesus, and you cannot live another minute without Him. Do you know The Author? Or if you have asked Him into your heart in the past, do you feel like its time to get sincere and humble yourself before Him. Ask Him to rescue you from the mangled mess of your reality. Humbly give over control of your decision making and ask Him to redeem your life. Or maybe it's time to ask Him, in splayed out honesty to forgive you for the casualties, the recklessness, the pain you've been responsible for…to forgive you. To heal you.

So today give him your broken roads, your dead ends, your messy meanderings. Give him your staggering shame, blinding failure. His glory on you will eclipse the former! His goodness toward you will astound you! It's time to turn the page, and move on from where you've been. *Your Story Is Not Done.*

Your old name no longer identifies you. The prison you've been in no longer holds you.

Son and daughter…son and daughter…

This is your time to meet The Author of your faith.

Please join me in this prayer:

"Father, I come to you as I am. I recognize how my sin has separated me from you. Please forgive me... I believe that your son, Jesus Christ died for my sins, was resurrected from the dead, is alive, and hears my prayer. I invite Jesus to become the Lord of my life, to rule and reign in my heart from this day forward. I don't want to do this without You anymore. Thank you Jesus that You had everything planned out for my needs to be met through the guidance of Your Holy Spirit. I commit the rest of my life to You. In Jesus' name I pray, Amen."

[3]

The Comeback Story

One of my favorite stories in the Bible is the parable of "The Lost Son." The story unfolds like a rich tapestry, and is a masterful explanation of God's plan of restoration for us no matter how far from home we've wandered. You may have heard this story called the "Prodigal Son." It is also referred to as the "Loving Father," and "Lovesick Father." The story found in the Gospel of Luke is a parable given by Jesus and recorded by his disciple Luke. Allow us to set the scene.

There once lived a wealthy and loving father who had two sons. The eldest had grown into a man. He was responsible, proven time and again to be trustworthy in running the family business when his father was away. He arose before sun up, and without being told went straight to his duties. Meticulous on details he prided himself on excellence. The father never had a moment's worry about his eldest. He was trusted. He was always dependable to the letter of the law.

The youngest son was the complete opposite. He was free-spirited dreamer, had a contagious laugh, and mischief seemed to follow him like his own shadow. Father and older brother always had to keep an eye on him to keep him focused. The relationship between him and old brother over the years had grown strained to say the least. The younger seeing his older as resigned, boring and stodgy. The older saw his young as a reckless brat getting away with everything. And if anyone was keeping tally, older bro was right, because most days he would have to put in extra work cleaning up little brother's mistakes, and finishing his chores for him. Each time, older brother would say to himself, this is the last time I clean up after you, But this time he meant it. That lazy, arrogant dreamer… thinks he's too good for hard work. He should have some priorities beat into him! I'm telling father I'm done cleaning up after him. It's time for him to grow up!

One especially beautiful spring day, the servant approaches the good father. The younger son has requested a word with him, and wants to talk as soon as he returns home from being out with his friends in the city. "Ah, yes, that's good." The Father thinks to himself, because I have something to talk to him about too. And yet the father's heart feels uneasy. Not only is he needing to have a tough love conversation about growing up and coming into responsibility, but he also has heard some scandalous rumors about this boy he's very concerned about.

Sadly, the rumors were true. The son's wanderlust was getting the better of him. He was feeling like a young stallion never let out of the stall. The best of life was passing him by! His friends were already sampling the high life in the big city. Why shouldn't he? He couldn't sleep. He had to get out! Experience life. Carpe diem! So he thought his situation over and came to a hasty decision. He decided to approach his Dad and ask for an early inheritance. I mean why not? 50/50 chance, right?

With wide-eyed hunger at a chance to spread his wings, the younger son gets ready to posture his opening statement with his father. With dramatic flare, he pitches his plea for how leaving the safety of home would force him to grow up. He always was a natural salesman.

The pitch was met with silence. Crickets... Startled by his son's request, the Father suddenly feels the air suck out of the room. Did he just ask me for his...inheritance? He blinks, waking out of the stupor. His mind aflutter with what he just heard, weighing the convincing argument to let him go early and live his life, find his path, but the sting of the timing... he was still so young in his father's eyes. A brief flashback danced across his memory of the boy at 6 galloping around the kitchen table like a wild stallion, squealing with delight, pretending he actually was a wild steed. He always did want to be free, thought the Father. Oh, my wild boy...

The Father's heart starts to ache, feeling the surge of worry. He has noticed his son's fancy toward fast living, that twinkle in his eyes talking about the mischief his friends are into and getting away with. The good Father feels his heart sink into his stomach. If I do cut him free, I may never see him again...but it's what he wants so badly.

Even though he won't be in the protection of my house, fed and cared for, and his livelihood it's all here, set up for him already. But...he doesn't want any of that. He wants out. Numb, the father succumbs to resignation. Over and over in his head he hears the painful truth: He doesn't want this... me, my love and protection anymore. Then graciously, with a shaky hand, the kind Father, hands the inheritance over to the son.

"Jesus continued: "There was a man who had two sons. The younger one said to his father, 'Father, give me my share of the estate.' So he divided his property between them.

"Not long after that, the younger son got together all he had, set off for a distant country and there squandered his wealth in wild living." Luke 15:11-13

The son—overwhelmed with freedom—lets his passion lead him wherever his heart desires. And over and over and over… he tastes forbidden fruit. Finds himself waking up in strange places in the perpetual "morning after." With stale breath, a ringing headache, a moment of concern would flutter through his conscience when he couldn't recall what he was doing the night before and with whom. The wild stallion was sowing his wild oats. And as the months passed, the son essentially blows the entire inheritance his father gave him.

Squandered. That word denotes a connotation of mishandling something and depending on where you're standing, just reading that word may even trigger a wave of guilt or shame. You may have had family and friends that counted on you, yet you blew it somehow. It may not be that your father gave you an early inheritance, but perhaps you had people who sowed love and time into you. Growing up, I went through periods of feeling as though I let everyone down. Being the youngest of two boys in my family, I can surely relate to this parable.

This verse in Luke depicts two things. One, the younger son blew it. He asked for an early inheritance and squandered it. But the other major point is that the father was more than willing to share his wealth at the drop of a hat. That is not common today among earthly parents. No father in his right mind would give his son a large early inheritance today.

The father was more than willing to give an early inheritance to his youngest son even though it was not something that was due him, at least not yet.

The story goes on to describe how the son began to squander the inheritance.

> **"After he had spent everything, there was a severe famine in that whole country, and he began to be in need. So he went and hired himself out to a citizen of that country, who sent him to his fields to feed pigs. He longed to fill his stomach with the pods that the pigs were eating, but no one gave him anything.**
>
> **"When he came to his senses, he said, 'How many of my father's hired servants have food to spare, and here I am starving to death! I will set out and go back to my father and say to him: Father, I have sinned against heaven and against you. I am no longer worthy to be called your son; make me like one of your hired servants. So he got up and went to his father." Luke 15:14-20**

I love how Luke describes the son waking up. "When he came to his senses." That's what happens to us. We go on and do things our own way, yet when things get hard and famine hits we finally come to "our senses" and long to turn to God.

The son hit hard times after wasting all the inheritance and began to remember how great it was to live in his Father's house. He began to long for that feeling of security of home.

Let's go there for a second. Try to remember when you were a child and you had no cares in this world. The innocence of being a child and knowing that your father and family were going to take care of your every need. Even if you did not have the best upbringing, chances are you still had your basic needs taken care of. That state of rest and faith in your family to take care of you is what Father God is wanting us to experience. He wants us to experience a full expectancy of Him. He wants us to feel secure in Him. That He will take care of everything. He will make a way where it seems to us there is no way! We just have to turn our hearts to Him and look to Him with child-like faith. In fact Jesus urges us to come to Him just like that. Like a child.

> **"He called a little child to him, and placed the child among them. And he said: "Truly I tell you, unless you change and become like little children, you will never enter the kingdom of heaven. Therefore, whoever takes the lowly position of this child is the greatest in the kingdom of heaven." Matthew 18:2-4**

Becoming like a child has two factors to it. Trust. Totally believing that your needs will be met by your heavenly Father...not event the faintest doubt crosses your thoughts. Because your heavenly Dad's track record has been consistent, He has always worked everything out. This is the understanding that God knows everything, sees everything and already has our answer. So we can believe that all the details are taken care of by Daddy God!

The second beautiful revelation about child-like faith pulls on your humility. Knowing that in your trust, you are fully relying on your Father to supply your every need. Today our society praises and promotes the notion of being independent and self-sufficient. The fact is simply this: Regardless of your age you must rely on God. It is humbling to think that you must rely on someone other than yourself to provide and sustain your livelihood and life itself.

If you read on in the above passage of Luke, you see that the son decides to humble himself, return back home and apologize to his father. Perhaps his father would have mercy on him and allow him back as a servant. He wisely realizes that even being a slave in his father's household would be a better life than what he was facing without him. That is the state of mind we need to have. Hard and fast living may have driven you to this point before; recognizing that you didn't know what you had until it was gone. But you don't have to learn those devastating life lessons by choice, you can humble yourself now and open your eyes to the perfect love of a heavenly Father, right in front of your face.

This posture of heart is called repentance. It requires humbling ourselves by turning away from our stubborn, head-strong way, and apologizing to our heavenly Father with a child-like heart. If you continue reading the parable you see the son does just that and begins his turn around by heading home. He decides to return to his loving father. And true to a masterful parable, the reunion delivers all the feels. The father is more than ready to receive him.

"But while he was still a long way off, his father saw him and was filled with

compassion for him; he ran to his son, threw his arms around him and kissed him.

"The son said to him, 'Father, I have sinned against heaven and against you. I am no longer worthy to be called your son.'

"But the father said to his servants, 'Quick! Bring the best robe and put it on him. Put a ring on his finger and sandals on his feet. Bring the fattened calf and kill it. Let's have a feast and celebrate. For this son of mine was dead and is alive again; he was lost and is found.' So they began to celebrate." Luke 15:20-24

How beautiful it is to see the father not just accepting the son back but at catching the first glimpse of him in the distance, the father actually takes off running toward him. There are so many rich details in the story to note! "But while he was a long way off..." so let your imagination go there for a minute!

The father clearly had been used to scanning the horizon regularly, for he caught him in eyesight while he was still a long way off. The father's heart skipping a beat at the mere image of his son's silhouette coming clearer into view. He probably rubbed his eyes to make sure he was seeing right. Everyday. Everyday he would stare off into the direction he last saw his son leave, holding onto a flicker of hope of seeing him again. The hopeful anticipation and the miracle had been realized in that moment! His son returned!

JORGE & KAT VAZQUEZ

In the distance, the son was taking in the familiar outline of the house coming into view…the fields…the crops were taller…*I hope older brother isn't around today, oh God, I…I don't know if I'm doing the right thing.* Surveying the horizon for a familiar face, his stomach in a hard knot, would he be cast out for good? Or maybe, just maybe accepted back somehow? Recently, his mind was consumed with guilt, shame and hopeless. Perhaps he had lost his family and they would never want to see him. He could never return to the same life.

Today you may be feeling in such a way. You may feel that you have lost your family for good. You may be feeling guilty for how things may have gone down or perhaps you may feel that you are way beyond misunderstood.

Shame is such a powerful emotion. It does not take much for our minds to muddle down the road of shame and regret. We all make mistakes, we all misspeak, or misrepresent who we are from time to time. By earthly nature, being human will take us down paths that will be filled with misunderstanding, arguments, and family rifts. All of which lead in the direction of shame.

But let me tell you that Jesus took all of our shame on the cross. He conquered death and part of that conquest was the shame that all of us who would place our trust in Him. You see, dwelling in shame leads to living your life like your dead already! It is a false filter placed on your life that makes you feel hopeless and undeserving of blessings.

Shame and its cruel step-sister, rejection, are powerful tools used by the enemy of your soul. They are tools Satan uses time and again to rob you of your true inheritance. You were created to love, be loved, and live an abundant life!

The father in the prodigal story ran after his son at the very first glimpse of his figure returning in the long distance. Recently we had friends staying with us. I was sharing how we were writing this chapter and my friends wife began to share her insights on this parable. She shared how in those days Jewish men wore long garments that carried to their ankles. She explained that it was shameful to reveal any a part of a person's leg. The fact that the father ran to his son meant that he had to lift up the garments to free his legs to run, thus taking on shame to reach his son. Isn't that a picture of what our Heavenly Father does through Jesus for us? He takes on our shame to reach us, to run after us at the very sight of our return to Him. So every time you feel shame or rejection try to creep back into you life, remember He paid the price so we can live free.

In the wake of the mess he had created for himself, the son realized he had lost any measure of good standing he maybe once had. That was his reality. And practically, the best he could hope for was that the father would allow him back in the household as a servant. That request came through a filter of shame. The perspective had reduced his hope and expectations for his life to be accepted back at the bare minimum of positions. In actuality the father was waiting and ready to restore him as a rightful heir in the family. He ran to him, embraced him, and to make an even bigger, more important statement, the father even more asked the servants to fetch two very important items. A ring and a robe. The father proceeded to place the ring on his son's finger which symbolized authority. Then, he wrapped a heavy robe around his son's shoulders, which represented righteousness. As if that wasn't message of acceptance enough, father's true *fullness of joy was going public! He had to share this happy reunion, it was news meant for celebration! And the father threw a welcome home party celebrating his son's restoration.

This masterful story told by Jesus, was unveiling the real story, a love story between The Divine and His beloved creation. That is the position we are found in when we return

41

to our heavenly Father through our Savior Jesus! God makes us heirs to His Kingdom, placing a robe of righteousness across our shoulders all because of Jesus' work on the cross.

"Now if we are children, then we are heirs--heirs of God and co-heirs with Christ, if indeed we share in his sufferings in order that we may also share in his glory." Romans 8:17

I delight greatly in the Lord; my soul rejoices in my God.

For he has clothed me with garments of salvation and arrayed me in a robe of his righteousness," Isaiah 61:10a

The shame Satan uses is the barrier desperately trying to blind and distract us from embracing that rightful position in God's family. Don't let shame or regret keep you from turning back to Father God. Remember Satan is the father of lies and the shame you've felt in your life is just a big fat lie meant to keep you from realizing that *you are royalty*!

Let's pick back up in the story, because it's not all daisies and buttercups. Not everyone is happy about the son's return home. The older brother. The Prodigal Son story sheds light into another dynamic going on at the same time of the joyful reunion: the older brother's real heart is revealed once he becomes aware that his younger brother has returned. The real smack in the face was that he actually was accepted back...and with fanfare by his father.

"Meanwhile, the older son was in the field. When he came near the house, he heard music and dancing. So he called

**one of the servants and asked him
what was going on. 'Your brother has
come,' he replied, 'and your father has
killed the fattened calf because he has
him back safe and sound.' "The older
brother became angry and refused
to go in. So his father went out and
pleaded with him. But he answered his
father, 'Look! All these years I've been
slaving for you and never disobeyed
your orders. Yet you never gave me even
a young goat so I could celebrate with
my friends. But when this son of yours
who has squandered your property
with prostitutes comes home, you kill
the fattened calf for him!'**

**"'My son,' the father said, 'you are
always with me, and everything I have
is yours. But we had to celebrate and be
glad, because this brother of yours was
dead and is alive again; he was lost and
is found.'" Luke 15:25-32**

As you see, the older brother reacts in anger at the news
that his brother is back home and is not only accepted by
his father but is being celebrated. His response is one all too
often common by some misguided Christians who react with
dismay when they hear of a prodigal one returning back to
Jesus after living a wayward life.

Take GRAMMY-winning, recording artist Kanye West's
profession of faith in Christ for example. The response by
some Christians has been skeptical at best and outright angry
at worst. Their argument is that Kanye in the past went so

43

far as to mock Jesus in his song lyrics. How can he be trusted, now calling himself a follower Christ? Yet their response shows their ignorance of God's game plan. They are missing the point of God's amazing grace. We can not earn God's love thus opening a door to be able to boast about it. It is totally a gift from Him who created us and longs to be with us.

I love the father's response to the older brother. He points to the fact that the older brother already has everything that is his: The property, the business, a future, food, and protection. Yet the younger brother was lost, reckless, and putting his life in danger. But now that younger son had been found and is now alive. That is the whole point of God's plan of salvation. He sent His son Jesus, who was both fully God and fully man, to live a perfect life here on Earth, solely to endure our sin on the cross in order to conquer death and give us life. The Plan was the ultimate love story, rescuing His creation from being lost.

I want you to know that God's desperate longing to reach and restore you is the entire theme of the Bible. Every story, parable, and scripture build up, and point to this resolution: God desperately wants you back. I want to quickly highlight two more parables that hammer this point home. The first is of the Lost Sheep.

"Now the tax collectors and sinners were all gathering around to hear Jesus. But the Pharisees and the teachers of the law muttered, "This man welcomes sinners and eats with them."

Then Jesus told them this parable: "Suppose one of you has a hundred sheep and loses one of them. Doesn't he leave the ninety-nine in the open

**country and go after the lost sheep
until he finds it? And when he finds it,
he joyfully puts it on his shoulders and
goes home. Then he calls his friends
and neighbors together and says,
'Rejoice with me; I have found my lost
sheep.' I tell you that in the same way
there will be more rejoicing in heaven
over one sinner who repents than over
ninety-nine righteous persons who do
not need to repent. " Luke 15:1-7**

Again there are two points to note that Jesus is making.

One is that despite having 99 other sheep, He is more than willing to leave them to go after the one that was lost. That means that despite all of those that already find themselves in the Kingdom of God, He is still looking for you to return home.

The next point was about who Jesus liked to hang out with. He was actually referred to a drunkard himself because he hung around with so many of them, not to mention "other sinners." The religious folk of the time couldn't stand it, and it drove the Pharisees nuts. This is the same attitude and posture you saw in the older brother of the Prodigal Son parable.

Today that is again what you see with some religious Christians. The point here is who cares what they say and think. Jesus the Master and Creator of the universe wants to reach you and hang out with you!

As if this parable wasn't enough Jesus immediately goes on to share another parable to deliver this concept.

**"Or suppose a woman has ten silver
coins and loses one. Doesn't she light**

a lamp, sweep the house and search carefully until she finds it? And when she finds it, she calls her friends and neighbors together and says, 'Rejoice with me; I have found my lost coin.' In the same way, I tell you, there is rejoicing in the presence of the angels of God over one sinner who repents."
Luke 15:8-10

Jesus was such a brilliant storyteller! Again here you see Him pointing out that God goes to great lengths to find those that are lost and more importantly will be rejoicing each and every time He finds them. That is the overall thread through all three of these stories. God wants to celebrate and rejoice every time He finds a soul that had lost their way!

My hope is that you are now found, and that you realize heaven has already thrown a major bash to celebrate your return home! If you haven't I pray that you would stop running and simply turn around to see that your Savior is standing there looking for you. He has been waiting for you, longing to catch a glimpse of you so that He can finally take off running towards you. His heart is busting at the seams over you, and as He embraces you, He wants to honor you, slipping the family ring on your finger and wrapping a robe of reestablished position around your shoulders. You are now home!

[4]

Epic Love Story

One of the earliest memories Kat has of being "in church" was when she was a little girl about four years old. This is her account: I remember the sights, sounds and feelings of one day in particular. It was a special occasion, the preschool Sunday school class was going to sing a song in front of the entire church. As the teacher paraded our giggly crew down the aisle to the stage, I remember the itchy, lacy, high-neck dress I was wearing that day feeling particularly tight and itchy, or was it her nerves?

Nonetheless, the electricity amongst the little friends standing at front of the sanctuary, on the stage was exhilarating. This was a view! The room hushed. We all looked over at the teacher, who with expressive eyes and a joyful surge of her arms signaled us to begin singing, "Jesus Loves Me." The chorus of high pitched voices fill the sanctuary. "Jesus wuvs me, dis I knoooow. For da Bible tells me sooooo." Fidgeting, twirling, dramatic waves of the arms, the teacher managed to direct us through the song and bring us all in for a landing, "Thaaaa Bible, tells, me soooo!"

I am sure you have heard this popular Sunday school song, and may have memories of singing it yourself. Yet the fact is that most people even those that grew up singing this song in church do not believe that Jesus truly does love them. We may not grasp that Jesus is sincerely, madly, deeply in love with us. Because we may have not had a parent or authority figure in our lives who genuinely was there for us, caring, protecting, nurturing and affirming us. We may not even have a grid for receiving unconditional love. But would you allow me to share with you the most remarkable and beautiful truth?

God is a hopeless romantic. As God is love, His capacity to love was so great He desired a creation to bestow His love on! Starting at the very beginning we can read in the book of Genesis He carefully and remarkably designed, gave destiny and purpose and above all, just wanted to love—to care for, to be in communion with—His creation. His love story began before the creation of time and has lasted countless millennia. It's what the Bible is all about, a love story of the Divine wanting to be in communion and in union with His Beloved.

I want to start by explaining Jesus' relationship with The Church. The Church is not a building, it is the collective of believers. The moment you put your trust in Jesus as your Lord and Savior, you are grafted into The Church.

Now The Church (God's people) plays a very significant role within the Kingdom of God. The collective of Believers is the human representation of a pivotal position on the Earth. The Church is described as The Bride of Christ, and correspondingly Jesus is the Bridegroom.

This may sound super weird to us who are men but it is a supernatural analogy that best describes the Love that Jesus has for His people—as well as the intimacy and unity He is seeking to have with us both on an individual and collective basis.

I want to highlight a verse that explains the dynamic of the relationship of Jesus and His Church. It is a verse in Ephesians that is instructing husbands to ensure they love their wives as much as Jesus loves the Church.

> **"Husbands, love your wives, just as Christ loved the church and gave Himself up for her to make her holy, cleansing her by the washing with water through the Word, and to present her to Himself as a radiant church, without stain or wrinkle or any other blemish, but holy and blameless. In this same way, husbands ought to love their wives as their own bodies. He who loves his wife loves himself. After all, no one ever hated their own body, but they feed and care for their body, just as Christ does the church- for we are members of his body.**
>
> **"For this reason a man will leave his father and mother and be united to his wife, and the two will become one flesh." This is a profound mystery but I am talking about Christ and the church. However, each one of you also must love his wife as he loves himself, and the wife must respect her husband." Ephesians 5: 25-33**

The relationship between The Church and Jesus is described as a "profound mystery." The fact that Jesus loves us so deeply as to prefer us over Himself is one that is pointed out as an example for earthly husbands to follow. We as earthly husbands need to go above and beyond to place our wives first in everything we do just as Jesus does with us, as The Church. But this love Christ has for The Church goes beyond that. As it stated He "gave himself up for her to make her holy." The Bible explains how Jesus paid the ultimate sacrifice for His ultimate love! He took on not only death on the cross, but all—and I mean *all*— of our guilt, shame, and sin so that we could be presented as holy and clean before The Father.

The picture I get here reminds me of a love story where a prince from a royal background meets a young lady with a troubled past. Insert your favorite love song here_____.

Boy notices girl. Their eyes catch in a double take. A wave rushes over him. She is lovely. The way her smile wrinkles up at one side…hooks him. Then he hears her laugh. A melody. The way her hair falls across her face, catches the sun and shimmers as it skims across her face. With a tilt of her head, she tucks it behind her ear. Then she glances his way once more. She noticed him! Her smile gives her away. That smile though.

The undertow of attraction, the swell of hope, the surge of chemistry when she's around him. She's all he wants.

> *"What can I do with my obsession?*
> *With the things I cannot see*
> *Is it madness in my being?*
> *Is it wind that blows the trees?*
>
> *Sometimes you're further than the moon*
> *Sometimes you're closer than my skin*
> *And you surround me like a winter fog*

You've come and burned me with a kiss

And my heart burns for you
And my heart burns"
"Obsession", Jesus Culture[1]

He has fallen for her and is completely obsessed. Yet. This love is forbidden. He knows she would not be accepted by his family with her past. The boy knows what he must do to erase her past. In a passionate and reckless plan of desperation, and in spite of his friend's strong objections, he carries out a plan that he knows would take care of everything. He would pay for the consequences from her past, expunging her record completely. Ignoring the fear that whispered that it wouldn't work, that he wasn't capable of carrying out the weight, he set his heart on getting her liberated from her record and thus free to unite with him in marriage.

That is our love story with Jesus! He wants to be with us so badly yet our sin is separating us from entering the Kingdom of Heaven. As a result He was willing to take on all of our consequences for our sin so we could live eternally with Him. Scripture shows us over and over again our position in this love story.

"I am jealous for you with a godly jealousy. I promised you to one husband, to Christ, so that I might present you as a pure virgin to him" 2 Corinthians 11:2

"You yourselves can testify that I said, 'I am not the Messiah but am

---

1 Smith, Martin. "Obsession." Consumed. Jesus Culture Music, 2009. Sparrow Records.

sent ahead of him.' The bride belongs to the bridegroom. The friend who attends the bridegroom waits and listens for him, and is full of joy when he hears the bridegroom's voice. That joy is mine, and it is now complete. He must become greater; I must become less."John 3:28-30

"However, as it is written: "What no eye has seen, what no ear has heard, and what no human mind has conceived"— the things God has prepared for those who love him."1 Corinthians 2:9

To enter into a relationship with Jesus shifts you into a new relational identity. You have been betrothed to Him as His Bride with Heaven as your home, and access to everything King Jesus died for you to have: Peace, hope, healing, joy and fullness of life. Everything your heart could ever need was already met in Him. I know that sounds simple, but it's true! That's a covenant promise, and He is aching to prove that to you when you run to Him first.

Even further, 1 Corinthians 2:9 gives us a sneak peak that our relationship as His Bride is as significant, deep, and ancient as time itself. The scriptures reveal that when we as the Bride of Christ realize who we really are, start believing it, thinking like it, we will start behaving like it! When we become Christians, the Holy Spirit literally takes up residence in our hearts. That triggers a process where we will start to learn how to submit our normal human-way of thinking and behaving how God wants us to think and behave as His beloved Church. This process takes place because He lives inside us now and we are learning how to function through Christ's character as citizens of heaven.

It will look like reaching out to the community around them, seeing the best in people through the eyes of supernatural love. This is how we can bring heaven's ways to earth, walking in forgiveness, being slow to anger, showing kindness and mercy, honoring others, reaching out, inviting those to our kitchen table who don't look like us, one person at a time.

This behavior the scriptures calls the awakening and manifestation of the sons and daughters of God. And it is essential for the fulfillment of prophecy that was older than time. How signifiant is our role as The Bride of Christ? The promises of God require it, the teaching of Jesus Christ requires it, the testimony of the Holy Spirit fulfills it, the destruction of Satan requires it, the vindication of Christ requires it, and the hope of the Saints demands it.

So you see, God's plans for you really are for you and His plans are greater than you can imagine! When we surrender, turning our control over to Him, give Him our heart, everything from there on changes. He will start healing your heart as you continue to trust Him with your decisions, inviting Him into the process. And He is a God of miracles, time has no effect on Him. He can turn your situation into your testimony! His plans are for you, to give you a great hope and future. And that is why I can sing "Jesus loves me. This, I know!"

[5]

David's Story

One of my favorite books in the Bible is Psalms. It was written mostly by one of the most fascinating and complicated individuals in history: King David. King David's story is so incredible it's kind of hard to believe it's true! He wasn't born into royalty, he was a shepherd boy and talented musician, and yet God guided him to become the King of Israel, a central figure in Judaism and Christianity. Dave's story gives us the hope that despite where you start, God can turn your story into the ultimate ending.

Because it all begins in the hill country of Bethlehem. Dave was already selected by God to lead a nation out of oppression and slavery. In the book of Samuel, you can read the set up. The current King of Israel Saul, failed to obey the Lord during a battle against the enemy tribe the Philistines. So God sent the Prophet Samuel to the small town of Bethlehem and guided him to Dave, who God was setting up to be the next King. But that was not exactly obvious at first.

The Prophet Samuel brought Dave back to Saul's courts, who upon hearing him play his music was so soothed, because scriptures tell us that Saul was "tormented by an evil spirit." Dave's music soothed the King. Saul was so taken with the humble young man that he would appoint him to be his armor bearer.

Soon after, a major Philistine battle loomed. The Philistines by the way were a tribe that included some giants. Yes, you read that right. God was setting up young Dave for a miracle that would live in infamy. God asked him to literally slay the giant Goliath, and Dave did without a blink in a miraculous fashion. As a result the heroic story about Dave spread throughout the region. An intense rivalry was brewing between the young new general and the king. End Chapter 1, turn the page to Chapter 2.

Could you imagine? From the hill country watching over sheep to the palace courts and being called the Slayer of Giants. What a whirlwind, right? Just as predestined, Dave would go on to take Saul's place as the King. He would meet fascinating people, wine and dine with influencers of the world and write more songs about it. He was noted for being the king who knew how to win battles, brought fusion between rival tribes creating a unified nation. His political and military achievements were sterling but his personal life was filled with conflict.

Here's the backstory. One day Dave was strolling on his rooftop terrace. From his viewpoint, he could see down to the street level and even into the neighboring buildings. Taking in the skyline, something catches Dave's eye… someone. Hmmm…who is *that*? In her outdoor jacuzzi, Bathsheba is taking a bath and Dave sees her…does a double take…and turns into a wolf. His animal instincts take over. He can't take his eyes off her. Dave falls hard. This woman. She quickly starts consuming his every thought, he can't sleep, he can't eat... such agony! But. She's taken. But Dave be like, "Who has time for reason when hormones are racing in my bloodstream?" She becomes his fantasy, the flame that torched his common sense. And he had to have her.

Dave compromised his reputation and began pursuing the captivating Bathsheba, who was already married to Uriah, one of his top commanders. But that didn't stop Dave. He sent for her. And Bathsheba later learns that she is pregnant. Oh snap.

But it wasn't just oh snap. In that culture Dave just crossed religious and legal lines: Pregnancy outside of marriage, and affair... these were grounds for stoning people to death. And not to mention he's the king of the land. Who unleashed this crazy mess? Yep. Dave did. Dave, the King anointed and appointed by God. He had to cover his tracks because it was spelling disaster with a capital D. We may have never gone there with our own lives, but at some level we can surely relate to dropping the ball. The feeling of *how do I get out of this mess I made for myself?*

He thoughtfully planned how to get what he wanted and still keep up "religious" appearances. Dave ordered poor Uriah to be placed in the front lines of a planned assault against the Ammonites, where he was instantly killed. Bathsheba went into her time of mourning, and after, Dave got what he was burning for: to marry her. Bathsheba gave birth to his son. But the Prophet Nathan sternly rebuked Dave for his evil scheming because it had "displeased the Lord." Sadly, their baby died.

Dave's life choices weren't perfect. They were effected by life, by longing, by loneliness, by need...and yet Dave found redemption in God's mercy. In fact, God called him, "a man after God's own heart." Now how's that for redeeming Dave and Bathsheba's hot escapade?

When you look up redemption in the Bible, Dave's picture should be there! Believe it or not, sex outside of marriage was not just a major no-no, in that culture it was punishable by the penalty of death. Having an affair, or even marrying someone else after a divorce was categorized as unlawful. Now before you check out, just track with me a minute and check *this* out: God was not blind-sided by any of this. He knew Dave would go crazy for another dude's wife and that he would plan to have the husband murdered. So now add murder to Dave's issues. That is some crazy stuff! Just jump inside Dave's mind and there's all the makings for a psychotic, steamy love song right there, forlorn lover who can't have the girl but makes some "plans."

So remember that word redemption? I can only imagine Dave and Bathsheba's consciences wouldn't let them sleep. Ever. Then enter Prophet Samuel with a stern warning and a terrible consequence of the anointed guy's outright offense, when he let his hormones lead. The loss of two human beings: Uriah, and Dave and Bath's first baby—not to mention how dishonoring his decisions had been to Bathsheba in the first place.

Dave was broken. Exhausted and utterly undone. He humbled himself. He got genuine before God. He asked forgiveness out of authentic repentance. Nothing would ease the pain knowing the mess he had created, nothing else—none of his dynasty's treasures, Cirque du Soleil performances or even tubs of Ben & Jerry's Chunky Munky ice cream would ease the feelings of pain and guilt, hide or make it better for Dave—only coming clean before God, facing the ugly truth, and asking forgiveness.

So when does God come in with Act 2, or even bring the rewrite to a mangled mess? To answer that let's look at the posture of Dave's heart at this critical cross roads moment of regret and lament. It's the posture of the heart, the authenticity that activates the rewrite. The Bible actually uses the word "supplicated," meaning a posture of genuine humility, David begged God earnestly for forgiveness. Earnest repentance leads to an exceptional rewrite!

Dave seemed like an all or nothing kind of guy...and God saw his heart was sincere. God can work with that! God in His unconventional ways where holiness meets the cross roads of mercy, heard their lamenting and their genuine prayers for forgivingness, and flipped their script!

But Dave and Bathsheba did go on to have other children—particularly a son, named Solomon, who would go on to fulfill prophecy! He completed the construction of the first temple, that his father had originally planned and began. Dave and Bathsheba's son Solomon would succeed him as king as well.

Dave was genuinely repentant. Knowing God's holiness is a promise He keeps, he acknowledged that his ways were dishonoring, covetous, selfish, borderline narcissistic, murderous, and careless with many hearts—even though he was the anointed King. Yet he earnestly begged for pardon. And God in, his never-ending love, knew He could work with a yielded heart. He even later called Dave "a friend of God."

The up's and down's of David's story can be felt in the songs he wrote (which can be read in the book of Psalms). He recognized that it was God who has rewriting the anthem of his life despite his failures. He writes:

"God rewrote the text of my life when I opened the book of my heart to his eyes." Psalm 18:24 MSG

Dave acknowledged that it was the hand of God who was behind the rewrite and redemption of his life. He had to trust and yield to allow God to re-author and edit his story. This required the king to come to God with sincerity, honesty, and a contrite heart. Dave wrote, "I opened the book of my heart to His eyes." The key was having his heart open and yielded to a rewrite by the Author of creation, God!

Watching God turn this tragic mess into a masterpiece can help you see areas in your life that God can rewrite. Why don't you ask the Spirit of God to help you. He's always looking for us to turn things over to Him in earnest repentance so He can rewrite our story. He specializes in amazing endings.

As a beautiful finale to Dave's redemption story, remember the other son he and Bathsheba had after he repented of his list of sins, Solomon…well he shows up in the lineage of Jesus Christ. How's that for a Rewrite!

[6]

A Dreamer's Story

The Biblical story of Joseph was about a real man who lived thousands of years ago. But his life could have been a script for a made-for-TV movie! Talk about the school of hard knocks: Joseph experienced the ultimate betrayal. He was sold into slavery by his own family, and later imprisoned although he was totally innocent. His life had all the elements of a perfect comeback story: From the pit to the palace! Yep, that's where he eventually ended up. But it all hinged upon Joseph's faith which was tested over and over again, growing stronger with each hard lesson. Because all he had was God and a dream.

Joseph's story is one that has been told and retold from generation to generation because it highlights the hope that we are given by God. Joseph's faith in God carried him through the craziness, the injustice and we have all experienced that in our lives at one time or another. His story is one that shows the true nature of God's heart to reveal, redeem and restore! The story of Joseph begins with a dream, an innocent mistake, and some haters!

> "Now Israel loved Joseph more than any of his other sons, because he had been born to him in his old age; and he made an ornate robe for him. When his brothers saw that their father loved him more than any of them, they hated him and could not speak a kind word to him.
>
> Joseph had a dream, and when he told it to his brothers, they hated him all the more. He said to them, "Listen to this dream I had: We were binding sheaves of grain out in the field when suddenly my sheaf rose and stood upright, while your sheaves gathered around mine and bowed down to it."
>
> His brothers said to him, "Do you intend to reign over us? Will you actually rule us?" And they hated him all the more because of his dream and what he had said.
>
> Then he had another dream, and he told it to his brothers. "Listen," he said, "I had another dream, and this time the sun and moon and eleven stars were bowing down to me."
>
> When he told his father as well as his brothers, his father rebuked him and said, "What is this dream you had? Will

61

your mother and I and your brothers actually come and bow down to the ground before you?" His brothers were jealous of him, but his father kept the matter in mind." Genesis 37: 3 -11

Joseph received a dream from the Lord that was so powerful and awe inspiring that he felt he had to immediately share it. But there was a problem. By sharing his dream, those around him began to get jealous. Typically, the people you want to share big things with are those who are closest to you: your family and close friends. Upon hearing your dreams and visions, usually among that same group, there may be some who get jealous, can't stand the idea, and go to work talking and dismantling your credibility, trying to cast shadows and limit your growth.

It is fallen, human nature for those around us to feel insecure when they see us striving, believing, and set for greatness. It's just a trigger mechanism that allows them to feel better about themselves by keeping others down in their place. It's simply insecurity.

Now that's not always the case. There are friends and family who are so secure in who they are in Christ that they will not try to limit you, but in turn be used by God to encourage and grow you. I want to encourage you today to drown out the noise of the haters! Remember the old saying, "Haters never win, and winners never hate!" Don't be limited by those around you who may love you, but due to their own insecurities would try to slow you down.

Today we have the social dynamic of virtual worlds. Social media and technology have built a platform that is fueled and driven by the powerful emotion of comparison and jealousy. Kat and I always discuss how the news industry is powered by fear. Kat has a journalism background, she was a news reporter for years. From time to time we would read a crazy headline or hear a story, shake our heads and repeat the old reporter's motto: "If it bleeds, it leads," meaning that fear attracts attention and drives ratings.

The same goes for jealously. Tech companies know this and have deployed thousands upon thousands of programmers and engineers to fine-tune algorithms to make it their job to keep you comparing yourself to other's, i.e., keeping you jealous of what others have or do. The whole strategy is intended to keep you glued to your screen, tumbling down an unending rabbit hole of comparison. So with this new dynamic feeding our thoughts. Because of screen intrusiveness, it is even harder to guard ourselves from the comparison trap, while staying focused on our unique dreams and callings.

After hearing Joseph's dreams, as well as seeing he was treated more favorably by his father, it was getting into the brothers' heads. To put it mildly: They were not only comparing themselves to their big-dreaming, hot-shot little brother who thought he was extra special, but with each day that passed, they started noticing that Joseph believed it! And that fueled their insecurity, fanning the flames of jealousy until it was an inferno of hate.

"But they saw him in the distance, and before he reached them, they plotted to kill him.

"Here comes that dreamer!" they said to each other."Come now, let's kill him and throw him into one of these cisterns and say that a ferocious animal devoured him. Then we'll see what comes of his dreams."

When Reuben heard this, he tried to rescue him from their hands. "Let's not take his life," he said. "Don't shed any blood. Throw him into this cistern here in the wilderness, but don't lay a hand on him." Reuben said this to rescue him from them and take him back to his father.

So when Joseph came to his brothers, they stripped him of his robe—the ornate robe he was wearing— and they took him and threw him into the cistern. The cistern was empty; there was no water in it." Genesis 37: 18-23

Joseph brothers became consumed with jealousy. Together, their half-jokes, talking-trash about bratty bro Joe turned more serious. It turned into a plot to kill him.

Insecurity and resentment fuel envy. Jealousy is such a powerful emotion that it can quickly begin to dominate and influence your thoughts. If you allow it to fill you, it will only lead to hate and despair. If left unchecked in your life, you too will live your life in a mental stronghold cycle of disappointment and jealousy: the hater lifestyle. However, one key thing to realize is that our Author can rewrite any story and as long as we trust in His direction. He can take haters and use them to propel your life into your destiny! He wants to free you,

As we continue on with Joseph's story, God softened the hearts of the brothers who once wanted him dead.

"As they sat down to eat their meal, they looked up and saw a caravan of

Ishmaelites coming from Gilead. Their camels were loaded with spices, balm and myrrh, and they were on their way to take them down to Egypt.

Judah said to his brothers, "What will we gain if we kill our brother and cover up his blood? Come, let's sell him to the Ishmaelites and not lay our hands on him; after all, he is our brother, our own flesh and blood." His brothers agreed.

So when the Midianite merchants came by, his brothers pulled Joseph up out of the cistern and sold him for twenty shekels of silver to the Ishmaelites, who took him to Egypt." Genesis 37:25-28

Just like in like in Joseph's story you may be facing a group who were as close to you as brothers, and now due to jealousy, they've turned on you with abnormal hate to the point that they almost wish you dead. Regardless what you may be facing, it is God who controls the heart of people. Just like in Joseph's situation where He turned their hearts from murder to allow room for him to escape, God can make a way for your good to come out of whatever situation you find yourself in. He can make a way where there is no way!

As we continue to see in Joseph's story, with God's favor he rose to the top to lead in every situation he was placed. From the pit he was sold to slavery. As a slave he began to run the household for his master Potiphar. Potiphar just happened to be a high ranking official in Egypt under the Pharaoh. Joe was about to get set up!

"The Lord was with Joseph so that he prospered, and he lived in the house of his Egyptian master. When his master saw that the Lord was with him and that the Lord gave him success in everything he did, Joseph found favor in his eyes and became his attendant. Potiphar put him in charge of his household, and he entrusted to his care everything he owned. From the time he put him in charge of his household and of all that he owned, the Lord blessed the household of the Egyptian because of Joseph. The blessing of the Lord was on everything Potiphar had, both in the house and in the field. So Potiphar left everything he had in Joseph's care; with Joseph in charge, he did not concern himself with anything except the food he ate."

Genesis 39: 2-6

When God is with you He will not only prosper you but He will even prosper those who bless you. So you see God blessed Potiphar because of Joseph.

Life started looking great for Joseph. He was given favor and a lot of opportunities and catching everyone's eye. In fact, he had caught the eye of his master's wife. Potiphar's wife was lusting for Joseph. She began to try to seduce him. And when he didn't respond to her advances, she would quietly wait, studying him, and planning her next opportunity—every one of which grew more brazen. She was pushing the envelope, especially for a woman of her stature.

Joseph continued to reject her advances, citing that it would dishonor his master who he greatly admired. In the flush of rejection and hormones, she grabs at him, her burning desire getting the better of her. Joseph breaks out of her hold and dodges her grasp, but she doesn't stop, she will not be rejected! She reaches out and snatches his robe. Joseph has barely broken free this time. But in a mixture of jilted love and panic, she devises a scheme to get him into trouble.

> "She called her household servants. "Look," she said to them, "this Hebrew has been brought to us to make sport of us! He came in here to sleep with me, but I screamed. When he heard me scream for help, he left his cloak beside me and ran out of the house."
>
> She kept his cloak beside her until his master came home. Then she told him this story: "That Hebrew slave you brought us came to me to make sport of me. But as soon as I screamed for help, he left his cloak beside me and ran out of the house."
>
> When his master heard the story his wife told him, saying, "This is how your slave treated me," he burned with anger. Joseph's master took him and put him in prison, the place where the king's prisoners were confined."
> Genesis 39: 14- 20

When you place your life in God's hand and are led by His Spirit, you will live in His favor. This favor could bring

JORGE & KAT VAZQUEZ

about jealousy in the lives of some around you and may bring some adversity. Just like Joseph, who found himself facing death in the bottom of a pit only to be rescued, he once again found himself bound (in jail) for doing the right thing. There can be great purpose even in pain, as we go through character molding that prepares us for the palace.

While in prison Joseph found favor with the prison warden and was promoted, being placed in charge of the other prisoners. You see, God used Joseph even during his imprisonment to be a blessing. And here is the game changer: We can shift our perspective of ourselves. By viewing yourself as a vehicle of blessing, God will use you to bless those around you, even in the middle of difficult situations. This perspective shift, is a decision we make reflecting our attention from ourselves and onto others' needs. A true trait of a leader is that he or she can be trusted to care for others!

And on a much larger view, it is during adverse situations that we as the Church must especially rise and shine, looking outside of ourselves, becoming a blessing to others and thus glorifying God!

As the story goes, God used Jospeh while in prison to interpret the dreams of two of Pharaoh's ex-officials: the cupbearer and the baker. The baker did not have a favorable outcome, however the cupbearer did. The cupbearer was eventually restored to his old position with the Pharaoh. Yet initially the cupbearer did not remember Joseph after moving back to the palace.

This is something that we as believers need to realize. When we do good to others, they may not reciprocate. It is not our duty to bless others in expectation of their blessing back to us. Our job is to bless as God has blessed us. This sowing will eventually bring about a harvest of blessing. Just like in nature, when a farmer sows the seeds, it takes a little time but the harvest comes. So will your harvest come as you live a lifestyle of blessing, living out being a blessing to others in Jesus name!

Eventually God delivered Joseph out of the prison, and this is when his destiny was revealed. God took him out of the prison and placed him in the palace. God again used Jospeh's talent of interpreting dreams to deliver him. All things really can work out for our good when we're called according to the Lord's purposes. Do you remember that cupbearer? Well check this out! Years passed, Joseph was still in prison but trying to make the most of things. Back in the palace, Pharaoh had a troubling dream and no one could interpret it. And the cupbearer, who Joseph had met in prison, remembered his old prison buddy who had a knack for interpreting unusual dreams. He sent for Joseph. His interpretation of Pharaoh's dream impacted the leader so much: Everything changed that night for Joseph. You never know when someone you made an impact on can be used by God to make an impact on your life!

> **"So Pharaoh sent for Joseph, and he was quickly brought from the dungeon. When he had shaved and changed his clothes, he came before Pharaoh. Pharaoh said to Joseph, "I had a dream, and no one can interpret it. But I have heard it said of you that when you hear a dream you can interpret it.""I cannot do it," Joseph replied to Pharaoh, "but God will give Pharaoh the answer he desires." Genesis 41: 14-16**

As you note above, Joseph always pointed out that it was God working through him, and not his own ability. As we go on using our God-given talents we must always be quick to point out how it is in fact God who is using us. Jospeh went on to interpret Pharaoh's dreams and as a result warned him of an impending famine.

> "It is just as I said to Pharaoh: God has shown Pharaoh what he is about to do. Seven years of great abundance are coming throughout the land of Egypt, but seven years of famine will follow them. Then all the abundance in Egypt will be forgotten, and the famine will ravage the land. The abundance in the land will not be remembered, because the famine that follows it will be so severe. The reason the dream was given to Pharaoh in two forms is that the matter has been firmly decided by God, and God will do it soon.

> "And now let Pharaoh look for a discerning and wise man and put him in charge of the land of Egypt. Let Pharaoh appoint commissioners over the land to take a fifth of the harvest of Egypt during the seven years of abundance. They should collect all the food of these good years that are coming and store up the grain under the authority of Pharaoh, to be kept in the cities for food. This food should be held in reserve for the country, to be used during the seven years of famine that will come upon Egypt, so that

the country may not be ruined by the famine." Genesis 41:28-36

God not only gave Jospeh the interpretation He gave him the wisdom and game plan to save Egypt. This was a major step in God's purposes to bring Joseph into his destiny. A destiny that in the end brings redemption and restoration. This too is his game plan for you as God is wanting to use you to bring about his redemption and restoration to the world!

> "Then Pharaoh said to Joseph, "Since God has made all this known to you, there is no one so discerning and wise as you. You shall be in charge of my palace, and all my people are to submit to your orders. Only with respect to the throne will I be greater than you." Genesis 41:39- 40

After being placed as Pharaoh's second in command, Joseph oversaw all the collection of 20% of the food, and supplies for the seven years of abundance that God had revealed to him in Pharaoh's dream. Once the seven years of famine came, his family back in Canaan (who were also facing famine) heard that there was provision in Egypt. They decided to go to trade for food as their situation had become dire. Little did they know that they were being setup for a family reunion with reconciliation and redemption written all over it.

> "Now Joseph was the governor of the land, the person who sold grain to all its people. So when Joseph's brothers arrived, they bowed down to him with

71

> their faces to the ground. As soon as Joseph saw his brothers, he recognized them, but he pretended to be a stranger and spoke harshly to them. "Where do you come from?" he asked. "From the land of Canaan," they replied, "to buy food."

> **Although Joseph recognized his brothers, they did not recognize him. Then he remembered his dreams about them and said to them, "You are spies! You have come to see where our land is unprotected." Genesis 42: 6-9**

Now all of a sudden after a tragic famine hits, the dream God gave Joseph manifests into reality. Through all the twists and turns, in the end God's promise through his dream came true—and it came right on time.

Just like God came through for Joseph, *He will come through for you.*

No matter what you are going through, God is going make a way where it may seem to you or others that there is no way.

> **But Joseph said to them, "Don't be afraid. Am I in the place of God? You intended to harm me, but God intended it for good to accomplish what is now being done, the saving of many lives. So then, don't be afraid. I will provide for you and your children." And he reassured them and spoke kindly to them." Genesis 42: 19-21**

Joseph had the choice to see his brothers picking up from when he saw them last: seeing their backs as they turned and walked away, feeling the sharp stab of betrayal and shock, intentionally leaving him in the pit. Or Joseph could capture this moment, and do something that went against all the old feelings.

Hindsight being 20/20, God certainly had worked His master plan out using the pit to promote Joseph into the palace with purpose to save an entire nation from a famine. Looking back over those 20 years, Joseph had witnessed a good Father working all things out for His higher plan. What the enemy had meant for evil, God was turning for good.

What Joseph's brothers did to him could have made him miserable, bitter, and self-destructive. But Joseph had been teachable. His character was bent, broken, humbled until all He had was his trust in God. That trust was the key. And as a result, God trusted him! He was used for a purpose greater than he could ever had imagined.

The character lessons he learned over those 20 years built up to one final test: one of the hardest lessons a human could face. Joseph's final test came down to the choice of showing mercy to his brothers the first time seeing them after his betrayal all those years ago. They were older, more worn and hunched over with the strain of the years, or could it be the 20-year burden they had carried. No matter, they were the ones that had intentionally left Joseph for dead. Time stood still for Joseph. How would he respond?

Joseph chose mercy. That level of mercy and forgiveness is the greatest lesson of all and is the stuff reconciliation is made of, where the impossible is possible again.

And isn't this the core of what love is? In spite of how we are treated, love never gives up. Never. Love hopes for all things, endures all things, forgives all things, and perseveres through all things. This is real love.

This is the kind of love Christ has for us—the kind of love that kept his feet walking up the hill to Calvary for us. We don't deserve forgiveness. But Christ loved us so much He went to the Cross for us and asked God to pardon our sins while we were betraying him, hating him in our hearts, hurting others, filled with selfishness. His mercy and goodness leads us to repentance and glorious new beginnings. That's where reconciliation and redemption are the impossible possibilities. What God did for Joseph, He can do for you: promoting you from the betrayal of being thrown into a pit to influential purpose.

What Jospeh did for his brothers, showing mercy, forgiveness and unmerited kindness, became the story told from generation to generation among Jacob's children and Joseph's family line. The mercy choice dismantled the power of evil's intent, reinstating in its place a level of love that became a glorious living blessing that would carry on in Joseph's family line. That generational mercy blessing manifested for an epic purpose in the life of one of Joseph's descendants who would come on the scene about 2,000 years later: Jesus Christ our Savior.

[7]

Stories from the Shipwreck

I love that the Bible isn't about a bunch of heroes, 10 feet tall and bullet-proof. They are real people navigating through life just like any of us. You may be stuck, your life is a poem, an ode to hopelessness. Your song is a lament. But there is still hope. God never leaves us—especially in the dark seasons of the soul.

Speaking of lament: The book of Lamentations gives us a peek into another interesting person in the Bible. The prophet Jeremiah struggled with depression and his thought life. You can read his diary in chapter 3. He was blessed with a gift of prophecy but still struggled with his thought life. But we read in Lamentations 3:1-24 that he coped by journaling and asked the hard questions of God. He believed God had caused his despondency. He writes:

> "I am the man who has seen affliction by the rod of the Lord's wrath. He has driven me away and made me walk in darkness rather than light; indeed, he has turned his hand against me again and again, all day long." Lam. 3:1-3

He experienced physical symptoms too.

> "He has made my skin and my flesh grow old and has broken my bones." Lam. 3:4

He felt trapped.

> "He has besieged me and surrounded me with bitterness and hardship.He has made me dwell in darkness like those long dead." Lam. 3:5-6

He kept on blaming God.

> "He has walled me in so I cannot escape; he has weighed me down with chains. Even when I call out or cry for help, he shuts out my prayer.
>
> He has barred my way with blocks of stone; he has made my paths crooked." Lam. 3:7-9

He thinks everyone is out to get him.

> "Like a bear lying in wait, like a lion in hiding, he dragged me from the path and mangled me and left me without

help. He drew his bow and made me
the target for his arrows. He pierced
my heart with arrows from his quiver.
I became the laughingstock of all my
people; they mock me in song all day
long. He has filled me with bitter herbs
and given me gall to drink." Lam.
3:10-15

He is in despair.

"He has broken my teeth with gravel;
he has trampled me in the dust.

I have been deprived of peace; I have
forgotten what prosperity is.

So I say, "My splendor is gone and all
that I had hoped from the Lord." Lam.
3:16-18

But take note in these next verses, because there's major
insight.

"I remember my affliction and my
wandering, the bitterness and the gall.
I well remember them, and my soul is
downcast within me." Lam. 3:19-20

Now there's a definite change in his thinking, a reversal
of his thoughts.

"Yet this I call to mind and therefore I
have hope." Lam.3:21

"*Call to mind.*" This is what we need to do, family. It's a shifting of how we look at things, turning from the negative to focusing on the positive. And for Jeremiah he arrests the inner monologue of negative thoughts and chooses to refocus, recognize and acknowledge that he is placing his hope in who God is and what he does. Game changer!

"Because of the Lord's great love we are not consumed, for his compassions never fail. They are new every morning; great is your faithfulness. I say to myself, "The Lord is my portion; therefore I will wait for him." Lam. 3:22-24

We could all follow Jeremiah's example and start refocusing our perspective. How do we position ourselves to receive God's rewrite? One practical way is to receive the truth and start believing it. A lot of us haven't even read that script yet because we've been buried in the first act, re-reading those lines over and over and over again.

Its so easy for the little frustrations to pile on top of the ever-recurring difficulties we just can't shake until we come to a boiling point. That's where a desperate inner prayer breaks out, "This is beyond me, I can't cope—it's consuming me—I can't rest—please help! God are you even there?"

Often when Kat feels buried, she runs to Psalm 23 in her Bible. The chapter talks of rest, serenity, strength, and calmness which bring healing and comfort in the face of frustrations. That chapter gives a character assessment of the One who can help Shepherd you out of the mess you feel lost in: the Holy Spirit. He makes real in us the very Presence of Jesus!

When we turn to Him, exposing the problem, acknowledging to Him its a tremendous difficulty...that's when He takes over in His own wondrous way! He applies the soothing, healing, answer of His own person and presence to my particular problem. Immediately we become aware of His dealing with the difficulty in a way that we may have not expected. And just like in Psalm 23, we are able to lie down in peace and rest because of what only Holy Spirit can do.

Further, another game changer in the middle of a muddle, has everything to do with asking the right question. We should be changing our perspective and asking, "What is it I need to call to mind?" Maybe, like Jeremiah, it's remembering God's blessings, His work and who He is.

When you're struggling, search for the blessings that are being overshadowed or ignored. It isn't denying the difficulties, but bringing a balance into our thought life.

Many of our emotional reactions depend on the story we tell ourselves. One practical exercise that gets us pointed in the right direction is to keep a journal. Monitoring your thinking, taking note on long you camp on an issue, and what your mood was during that time is very insightful. There is so much to learn from the patterns you will pick up.

Kat has a habit of posting little scripture cards all over the place. They're little post-it notes with Bible promises written on them and then I hear her literally speak those out loud, like a declaration. Over the years she has accumulated verses that remind her of her identity as God's child, and what God tells us to meditate on. Here are a few of her favorites:

True Thoughts

I am secure.

> **I can rest knowing His plans for me are good, to give me a hope and future. (Jeremiah 29:11)**

I can trust Him because He helps me. (Psalm 28:7)

I am assured that God works to ensure my good in all circumstances. (Romans 8:28)

I have not been given a spirit of fear, but a spirit of power, love, and a sound mind. (Romans 8:37)

I am accepted.

I am God's child. John 1:12

I am complete in Christ. Colossians 2:9-10

I have been chosen by God and adopted as His child. Ephesians 1:3-8

I have been redeemed and forgiven of all my sins. Colossians 1:13-14

I am significant.

I was known by God before I was even formed in the womb, set apart and appointed. Jeremiah 1:5

I am God's handiwork, created in Christ to do good works, which God prepared in advance for us to do. Ephesians 2:10

I am confident that God will complete the good work He started in me. Philippians 1:6

I can do all things through Christ, who strengthens me. Philippians 4:13

Challenge: Retraining your thoughts

Football coaches are able to challenge the ruling of a play and often the decision is reversed. These challenges have made the results much more accurate. You and I have the same freedom and opportunity to challenge the truth of what's playing over and over in our thought life.

We're going to challenge our thought life for accuracy: how do our real thoughts measure up against who God calls us to be, how we are to believe, think and behave. Because we want to help you renew your mind and remind your own ears of the truth, let's try an experiment.

1. Grab your journal and keep a summary of thoughts that feel restrictive and toxic.

Write down what the thought was.
What is the proof that supports it?
Whats the evidence that doesn't support it?
What do I do now?

If you're like most of us, you've spent years training your mind. The constant repetition of negative self-talk can create negative thinking in our brain. If you've had a thought once, then there's no effect but what if you've thought about it thousands of times over the years?

I often describe our thought life like driving on a road. Driving on a stretch of brand new asphalt makes for a smooth ride. But months and certainly years later, ruts, pot holes, ridges wear into the road from tires rolling over the same path thousands of times. The makings for a bumpy and not so peaceful ride.

Your goal is to develop a new, healthy foundation filled with truthful thoughts so you can make peace with your mind.

2. Now let's create a list of truthful statements about yourself.

Go get a Bible, and start writing out some key scriptures as your declaration. You can use the list under the above section "True Thoughts." In Kat's book *REIGN: Restoring Identity*, she also has a more expanded list of powerful Bible promises used to remind ourselves of the truth.

The weird part comes now, but we're retraining our thoughts, remember? Once you have written them out, we want you to start declaring them out loud, reminding your ears of the truth. Speak it, shout it, sing it until you believe it!

Here's where we can start retraining our brains to believe it. Because it's scientifically proven that it takes repetition to develop a new habit, we are challenging you to take the next steps to start that process and commit to putting it into practice over and over. Select a few scriptures that refute the original "pot hole" thought you've been believing for so long. Read and speak out loud those scripture truths to yourself several times a day. When its audible, especially when you hear your own voice, the new thought gains a greater foothold. Here is our new confession, please declare this out loud with us:

Identity Declaration

"I am loved by the Father. I am adored by the Father. I am approved of by the Father. He finds pleasure in me. He calls me

YOUR STORY IS NOT DONE

capable. He calls me worthy. I am greatly valued. I am treasured by the Father. I am a child of The King! Today, I receive His great love for me."

This is how we retrain our brains to start believing not just truth—but the biggest game changing truths: God is in love with you, is so proud of you, and has wonderful plans for you!

Jesus conquered the cross, hell, and the grave. His speciality is comeback stories! It's time to start believing the goodness of God in your circumstance and in your life and lining up your thoughts and words in faith. Believe it. Your test will become your testimony.

"For I know the plans I have for you," declares the Lord, "plans to prosper you and not to harm you, plans to give you hope and a future. Then you will call on me and come and pray to me, and I will listen to you. You will seek me and find me when you seek me with all your heart." Jeremiah 29:11-13

[8]

New Story

Are you ready for your story to change? Are you ready to be reinvented?

How about being recreated? The moment you trust Jesus to take over your life and begin letting Him rewrite your story, you become a new person. The trajectory of your life is reset and you are given a gift of brand new life. The Bible calls it being made alive! Now this life won't be all sunshine and buttercups while you are still on earth, but it is one that will be filled with His peace because He literally will be residing in you. And here's an even larger perspective: you will live forever! Because your sins have been forgiven, one day you will have eternal life in heaven. It is by God's amazing grace and deep love for you!

With Jesus Christ in your heart, He is in you literally, and the Bible says something profound to prove that He really does have everything your heart could need.

"But because of His great love for us, God, who is rich in mercy, made us alive with Christ, even when we were dead in our trespasses. It is by grace you have been saved! And God raised us up with Christ and seated us with Him in the heavenly realms in Christ Jesus, in order that in the coming ages He might display the surpassing riches of His grace, demonstrated by His kindness to us in Christ Jesus." Ephesians 2:4-7

The scripture tells us that because of His great love, once we ask Jesus into our hearts some magnificent—and miraculous—things immediately begin to happen. He lifts us up with Christ, seating us with Him, so we have access to everything our heart could need. It's His Kingdom! His Kingdom is righteousness, peace, and joy. We can have peace *now* because He is in us. We can have joy *now*. No matter what our circumstances, we begin to realize the Jesus really is rewriting our story.

One of the first lines of your new story is your coming to Him and acknowledging He is the only Lord of your life. So now you can begin a life-long conversation with God (called praying—or just talking with Him) about your needs and situations in your life. You can trust Him because He will give you the answers you need. And the result of that is how you stay full of peace. This is the goodness of our Father. He is a promise keeper. You can trust Him because Jesus died and is risen for us.

Yielding to the Lordship of Jesus Christ is a humbling and life changing decision.

But He promises as you release your burdens and trust Him, He makes all things new. Your life, your dreams, your purposes will be all be reformed and restored under His perfect love and through His grace. You will experience a peace—a "foundness"—with waves of love melting over you like never before. Experiencing His love is so hard to describe in words. But it's *real* and ***transformational***.

As you receive His love, He is also synchronizing the beat of your heart with His. Because He is your Father and you are his child, the same love will start to course through your veins too. You will start to see others as He sees them, just as He sees you…redeemed. This is how you know He is transforming you. You will become a catalyst of blessing to yourself and others. The Bible describes this transformation in 2 Corinthians:

> **"Therefore, if anyone is in Christ, the new creation has come. The old has gone, the new is here!" 2 Corinthians 5:17**

You are now in Christ relationally, which also means you are part of His Body, the church. Things will never feel the same, sound the same, or be the same. He is part of you. You have your Daddy's eyes and heart now. I love how the Amplified Bible delivers this point:

"Therefore if anyone is in Christ [that is, grafted in, joined to Him by faith in Him as Savior], *he is* a new creature [reborn and renewed by the Holy Spirit]; the old things [the previous moral and spiritual condition] have passed away. Behold, new things have come [because spiritual awakening brings a new life]." 2 Corinthians 5:17 AMP

Eternity. It's the best part of your story because you have a new ending that can have no end. Death comes to all of us—but those who put their faith in Jesus live forever.

That truth is foreshadowed every day. The foreshadowing is manifested by how you are experiencing His peace. Others around you will begin to recognize that somehow you are different as they see you walking in His peace and making new choices that demonstrate that.

Next you will begin to lose the hunger to do things you used to do that are destructive. As you grow in your faith and walk with God, you will lose the appetite to do things that lead you away from Him. After encountering Jesus you now have a spiritual awakening that "brings new life." His Holy Spirit now lives in you and He will guide your steps.

Lastly you are made righteous. The Bible is clear that no one can be made righteous on their own merit or strength. You can not earn your way into heaven nor into right standing with God. It is impossible, yet with God all things are possible. Jesus has made a way where there was no way to make you righteous before God.

> **"But now apart from the law the righteousness of God has been made known, to which the Law and the Prophets testify. This righteousness is given through faith in Jesus Christ to all who believe. There is no difference between Jew and Gentile, for all have sinned and fall short of the glory of God, and all are justified freely by his grace through the redemption that came by Christ Jesus." Romans 3: 21-24**

Now all of the pressure to perform or live up to a holy standard are gone.

We are made righteous and are saved by God's grace, which has come through Jesus and our redemption that came through His cross. This gives us freedom from death and freedom to serve God with humility and gratitude. He has made a way for us to be in right standing with Him. He has given us a new story. In fact God has taken it a step further than just having us be in good standing with Him, He actually has *adopted us as sons and daughters.*

"For those who are led by the Spirit of God are the children of God. The Spirit you received does not make you slaves, so that you live in fear again; rather, the Spirit you received brought about your adoption to sonship. And by him we cry, *"Abba,* Father." The Spirit himself testifies with our spirit that we are God's children." Romans 8:14-16

God loved us and wanted to be with us so much that He not only sent Jesus to die on the cross for us, He actually made a way to have us adopted into His eternal royal family.

Every time I read this passage in scripture I am reminded of a conversation I had years ago with one of the other fathers on my son's soccer team. The dad was telling me the story of their son who was adopted.

They had two other children by natural birth and the third son was adopted. He told me how it took a few years and court battle after battle to fight to gain the right to adopt their son.

He said it was the battle of his life, but they did everything that it took and gave everything to ensure they could adopt their son! I think that's a perfect picture of what Daddy God did for you and me. He fought and gave everything, even His only begotten Son, to ensure we were adopted into His family!

And now that we are adopted into God's royal family, we have been given not just eternal life, but heavenly, supernatural benefits and access while here on earth. That same passage in Romans goes on to explain our new found position:

> **"Now if we are children, then we are heirs—heirs of God and co-heirs with Christ, if indeed we share in his sufferings in order that we may also share in his glory." Romans 8:17**

We were made to rule and reign with Jesus in God's Kingdom. Our adoption into sonship means He is giving us authority to take back dominion on earth for His Kingdom ways. The Lord's prayer proves as we read Jesus' words in Matthew 6:10, "Your kingdom come, your will be done, on earth as it is in heaven." Who do you think He uses to carry out His will being done on Earth? His children who hear His voice. We are called to carry out His purposes on Earth as it is in heaven.

> **"And God raised us up with Christ and seated us with him in the heavenly realms in Christ Jesus," Ephesians 2:6**

The word "rule" is defined as control of or dominion over an area. "Reign" means to hold and carry out a sovereign office. So our positions as God's adopted sons and daughters is a position of great impact, which has everything to do with our new found heavenly, royal bloodline. We are entitled to Kingdom authority. It's a legitimate right that comes with the territory (so to speak). It is now part of our new story.

To explain the unique authority we carry as Believers, Kat often explains it like a sheriff and outlaw showdown that you know from those classic Western movies? In her book *REIGN: Restoring Identity* she shares, "There was always that one scene, normally the climax of the movie where the sheriff faces off against the outlaw. You know the one, the scene filmed in front of the saloon, usually meeting at "high noon," called the showdown scene between sheriff and outlaw. Sheriff facing due east, outlaw facing due west, pace off 10 steps in opposite directions, and then spin around on their jingling boot spurs. Lightning-fast they reach for their holsters, whipping out the Colt .45 and unleash fury on each other. They both show courage but normally the sheriff would prevail." And the Sheriff ensures peace and order back to the little town.

The classic showdown scenario is a great example of who carried the legal right to enforce the law in the town. Both sheriff and outlaw carried power, the Colt. 45, but only one held legal right to enforce the law. Anyone breaking the law has to comply to the law officer or face the consequences. This same principle can be applied to us, as we see our true identity in Christ. We believers carry heavenly authority. So what does this mean practically for us as Christians? We can see countless scriptures in the New Testament where Jesus' divine rights were demonstrated in his earthly ministry. His authority was active to heal, to free people from lies, and walk in supernatural love.

At the point of salvation, positionally we are in Christ, seated with Him in heavenly places. All demonic powers are under His feet.

"Praise be to the God and Father of our Lord Jesus Christ, who has blessed us in the heavenly realms with every spiritual blessing in Christ. For he chose us in him before the creation

of the world to be holy and blameless in his sight. In love he predestined us for adoption to sonship through Jesus Christ, in accordance with his pleasure and will." Ephesians 1:3-5

"The Son is the image of the invisible God, the firstborn over all creation. For in him all things were created: things in heaven and on earth, visible and invisible, whether thrones or powers or rulers or authorities; all things have been created through him and for him. He is before all things, and in him all things hold together. And he is the head of the body, the church; he is the beginning and the firstborn from among the dead, so that in everything he might have the supremacy. For God was pleased to have all his fullness dwell in him, and through him to reconcile to himself all things, whether things on earth or things in heaven, by making peace through his blood, shed on the cross." Colossians 1:15-20

Also when we accept Him as Lord into our hearts the Holy Spirit comes into us, and we are adopted in sonship to the Body of Christ.

"Just as a body, though one, has many parts, but all it's many parts form one body, so it is with Christ," 1 Corinthians 12:12

Christ is the head of the Church and we are His Body. So that means we are the bearers of The Firstborn's (Jesus') power and authority, as we are in Him and He is in us. We are now His ambassadors on earth.

There is a difference in having authority bestowed upon us: we are beholding to His higher law. Our rule is God's love. As we were changed into His likeness and image when we become followers of Christ, our new royal position activates a purpose. We will be used to free people from darkness and reflect His nature. Our hearts will synchronize with His, and we will be transformed in how we see others because He literally is living inside us now. Through His loving perspective, He sees people restored and set free, with heaven living inside of them here on Earth. If we put His love glasses on, we not only will recognize the changes in us, our new storyline unfolding, but will be able to see the changes in others as well.

Our new position came at the most expensive price: Calvary's Cross.

When we accept His amazing gift of grace and the forgiveness of our sins, we become His adopted children and heirs. It all becomes relational. We are His, with a divine imprint on our hearts, meant to bring His kingdom to Earth. The heavenly authority we carry reflects the truth that we are not our own. We were called to this. We were created for this. He paid the price for this. We were called to rule and reign with Him.

[9]

The Rewrite

Rewrite is to write something again to alter or improve it. Also known as editing in the literary world, rewrites also have implications in the abstract world of math, logic and absolutes. Rewriting in computer science for example covers a wide range of methods for replacing sub-terms of a coding formula with other terms. These are called rewriting systems, and for those of us learning this concept for the first time, their most basic form consists of "a set of objects, plus relations on how to transform those objects," according to Definitions.net. One rule to rewriting a term (pardon me as I get mathy) could be applied when it's combined to a particular algorithm and totally transforms a computer system, impacting the entire program's language. That's geek-speak for a new system is running!

I love the computer programming definition of rewrite. Sub-terms of a formula are replaced with other subordinate terms. And here is another mind-blowing fact to land on.

The definition of sub-term is a position "under the power or authority of another." You know where I'm going with this, right? Once we surrender our control over to a loving Savior, He rewrites our story! And once you add in His eternal "algorithm," He recreates our thinking, behavior, and purpose entirely. That's a mathematical formula for transformation!

Abiding. Something Kat and I try to do everyday is have abiding time with the Lord in the mornings. Starting our day in a rendezvous with a very real God just sets the day in a "right" flow. It has been a game changer for our relationship with Him because He wants to engage us in every detail. This critical quiet time with the Lord is something that I learned from a mentorship program led by Ed Kobel. Normally after we read God's Word and have a devotional and prayer, we carve out time to intentionally quiet our hearts and press into his Presence. This is individual time one-on-one with the Holy Spirit. And we have a journal and pen ready because once the conversation opens up He talks back!

Sometimes we can right off ask, "Father, how do you see this situation, or how do you see me?" Get ready to dictate what He tells or shows you. He is so ready to show Himself personally and intimately to you and your situations.

At other times He will give you a word, a song lyric, a poem, a love letter, an impression, an idea, or bring up a conversation or memory. It's never in shame or judgment, but always washed in gentleness and love. He will answer you. As we have made notes or even sketched out what He was communicating to us during that time, abiding has proven to us how personal and real a Father He is and how He is genuinely for us. The full effect of abiding comes as you endure, staying fixed and intentional in his conversation with you until He is finished. One thing that Ed encouraged us to do is press into that time with the Lord until you feel He dismisses. It's like when your favorite love song comes on and you're interrupted a minute into the song. Well, that's no good. It ruins all the feelings the song evokes. A good love song deserves to be heard to the end! Especially Extreme's "More Than Words," as Kat would say! Whenever that song comes on she hushes anybody standing around in reverence to the moment.

That's the same concept as abiding with Him. He wants to sing His love song to you. He wants you to experience all the wonderful emotion of "sweeping you off your feet"! This is where deep heart healing happens and quickly this intimate time with Him, because He is a true romantic, you will develop a clearer and clearer hearing heart, able to hear His voice and know Him more intimately. Transformation happens here, on how He really sees you and how He wants you to see others. Our hearts are synchronizing with His.

As we rest in who He is, praying for our decisions to line up with His will and trusting Him, our spirits are recharged and renewed. It's a total release. Activated trust! And abiding means accepting which activates our humility. For in our weakness, He is made strong!

In this dance of surrender, abiding in Him is a key to navigating the real relationship you have with Him. Abiding means to stay stable, fixed in a state of love. It's an opportunity for Him to perfect love and joy in us.

You may be asking yourself, "Can I really hear God? Is it really possible for me to hear His voice?" The answer is an emphatic *YES*. I want to show you in scripture where Jesus explains this simple truth of having the ability to hear and be led by His voice.

"The gatekeeper opens the gate for him, and the sheep listen to his voice. He calls his own sheep by name and leads them out. When he has brought out all

his own, he goes on ahead of them, and his sheep follow him because they know his voice. But they will never follow a stranger; in fact, they will run away from him because they do not recognize a stranger's voice." John 10: 3-5

Now that you have received Jesus as your Lord and Savior, you are placing your trust in Him. You have received his Holy Spirit and thus are being led by Him. This means you will be able to hear Him and you will be able to follow His lead as He rewrites your story. You will no longer follow strangers onto a destructive path. You will be led into safety of the gates to God's kingdom— experiencing His peace, joy, love, and hope! Jesus goes on to double down on this point:

"Therefore Jesus said again, "Very truly I tell you, I am the gate for the sheep. All who have come before me are thieves and robbers, but the sheep have not listened to them. I am the gate; whoever enters through me will be saved. They will come in and go out, and find pasture. The thief comes only to steal and kill and destroy; I have come that they may have life, and have it to the full.

"I am the good shepherd. The good shepherd lays down his life for the sheep. The hired hand is not the shepherd and does not own the sheep. So when he sees the wolf coming, he abandons the sheep and runs away.

Then the wolf attacks the flock and scatters it. The man runs away because he is a hired hand and cares nothing for the sheep.

"I am the good shepherd; I know my sheep and my sheep know me— just as the Father knows me and I know the Father—and I lay down my life for the sheep." John 10: 7-15

Jesus describes Himself as the "Good Shepherd." Just like sheep recognize and follow their shepherd's voice, we as believers will hear His voice, recognize it, and then follow Him. The more time you spend with the Good Shepherd, the easier it is to recognize his voice. There are primarily two ways to do this: One is through reading God's Word; the other is through real prayer.

The Bible is the infallible Word of God and is the best way to train yourself to recognize his voice. God will speak to your heart in a still small voice as you begin to spend time with Him in prayer.

The key to recognizing His voice is to know His voice in scripture. In fact there are two Greek words for the Word of God. One is *Logos*, the eternal word of God. This is the word used when describing the Bible. The other is *Rhema*, or fresh Word of God. This is the word used when describing God speaking to someone. The Rhema will always line up with the Logos. I always use this analogy when teaching others how to hear the voice of God. Imagine that you are on a boat with your friends in the ocean. While you are not looking a wave jumps up and splashes you in the face. You have water all over your face. How do you discern that the water came from a wave and not your friend splashing you with a water bottle? You can taste it…it's salty and not fresh water. You didn't have to see it come from the ocean to know that it did indeed come from the sea. The consistency of the taste lined up with what you knew already to be true about ocean water. So it is true for God's word. As you study and know God's Logos you will easily recognize the Rhema He speaks to you as it will line up with His Word. As God speaks to you He will never ask or show you something that goes against His Word in Scripture.

I want you to know that as a Believer you are called to be a disciple of Christ. I am sure if you grew up around church or churchy people you have heard that term before. But I want to give you a better definition. A *disciple of Jesus* is simply a follower of Christ that hears His voice and does what He says.

I believe the key to this is staying connected to Him and abiding in Him.

As I mentioned earlier, I recently finished a mentorship program with a very successful businessman named Ed Koble. Beyond being responsible for managing billions of dollars worth of real estate, he has also devoted his life to teaching believers how to abide in Jesus, how to hear their Shepherd's voice and how to follow His character bearing fruit of love, joy, peace, and hope.

One principle he discusses is that of abiding time we described above. Spending time just listening to God and journaling what He impresses on your heart. Like dictating! Taking Scripture and asking God probing questions that allow Him to lead you deeper into Him. The key is taking that time out consistently. Staying connected to God each and everyday is a vital relationship which leads to great fruit. I believe that is true discipleship as we read in John 15:

"I am the true vine, and My Father is the vinedresser. Every branch in Me that does not bear fruit He [a]takes away; and every *branch* that bears fruit He prunes, that it may bear more fruit. You are already clean because of the word which I have spoken to you. Abide in Me, and I in you. As the branch cannot bear fruit of itself, unless it abides in the vine, neither can you, unless you abide in Me.

"I am the vine, you *are* the branches. He who abides in Me, and I in him, bears much fruit; for without Me you can do nothing. If anyone does not abide in Me, he is cast out as a branch and is withered; and they gather them and throw *them* into the fire, and they are burned. If you abide in Me, and My words abide in you, you will ask what you desire, and it shall be done for you. By this My Father is glorified, that you bear much fruit; so you will be My disciples." John 15:1-8 (NKJV)

Here you see that God is wanting you to abide or remain (NIV) in Him. He is looking for you to bear much fruit. The fruit of peace, love, joy, and hope. By bearing much fruit you will show that you are His disciple. The only way to do that? It's very simple, just by spending more personal time in His Word. Engage Him in prayer, and allow Him to speak to you. Give Him the right of way to lead and guide you as He rewrites your story!

[10]

Share Your Story

Clean slate. Fresh start. Now you have a brand new story, a brand new life, and you have been literally recreated by the Author and Finisher of life itself—Jesus! So what's next? Glad you asked. Now it's time to share your story.

Your story is amazingly powerful. It is a testament to God's engagement in your life. And just as we look to powerful stories like Joseph to encourage us, people will start to look to your story to be encouraged. What God is doing for you He also wants to do for others. It's up to you to share that awesome truth.

God is in the story-telling business. Just look at the 66 books of the Bible.

It is filled with story after story that tell of His might and grace, and His plan to save us and rewrite our stories through Jesus. Story is the way that He paints the picture of His plan. And now you are part of that plan!

A God written story is so powerful. In fact, there are two main ingredients in overcoming satan. The power of Jesus' blood and your story! You see your story is a testimony and it is part of the equation to defeat the enemy. In the book of Revelation John writes:

> **"And they overcame him by the blood of the Lamb and by the word of their testimony, and they did not love their lives to the death." Revelation 12:11 (NKJV)**

This short but power-packed verse gives you a blueprint to overtake any attack from satan. But it's not a plan only for you, it is also for others. You see your story and the precious blood of Jesus are the way that others will find victory in their lives. I love how the New International Version of the Bible translates this passage.

> **"They triumphed over him by the blood of the Lamb and by the word of their testimony; they did not love their lives so much as to shrink from death." Revelation 12:11**

"They triumphed..." Mic drop! And chill bumps! Can't you just feel the surge of victory and freedom after reading that? Relish that feeling because its warranted: Jesus just rewrote your story—that is radical grace! That feeling is meant to be shared. You have a secret weapon that is meant for you to use to help free others from the oppression and lies from the enemy.

Sound heavy? It's really quite simple. All you have to do is share what God has done for you with the people who cross your path, because its the same thing He wants to do for them. *Just show up and share!*

So imagine it like this, like going through a world-wide pandemic. What if you had the cure so that no one would have to suffer loss of life from the virus? Today we are facing a crisis far greater than any health pandemic in history. The world is facing the sickness of sin that slowly, but surely, robs individuals of their joy, peace, and ultimately leads them to an eternal death.

> **"For the wages of sin is death, but the gift of God is eternal life in Christ Jesus our Lord." Romans 6:23**

However you know and have experienced the one and only true cure. You have experienced Jesus and His precious Blood. He rewrites stories, restores peace in our hearts, and gives us the gift of eternal life. You have the ability to share your personal story of how you experienced His healing hand in your life. And you know how others can too. Just like you heard the stories of persons being set free by Jesus, you can share so they too can find the Cure. There is *power* in your story. It is the Good News and *you* are called to declare it. In fact, Jesus told us to!

> **"And then he told them, "Go into all the world and preach the Good News to everyone." Mark 16:15 (NLT)**

Jesus is calling us to go and share this awesome Good News. There is a cure to the worst disease man has ever experienced: sin, torment, and spiritual death. There is away to escape, all while being restored to how we were meant to be: one people in union with our one, true God! This is Jesus' commission for us to be His hands and feet by sharing the

Gospel through our story. In Mathew we read where Jesus is commissioning His disciples to go and do the very thing He is calling you and me to do.

> **"Then the eleven disciples went to Galilee, to the mountain where Jesus had told them to go. When they saw him, they worshiped him; but some doubted. Then Jesus came to them and said, "All authority in heaven and on earth has been given to me. Therefore go and make disciples of all nations, baptizing them in the name of the Father and of the Son and of the Holy Spirit, and teaching them to obey everything I have commanded you. And surely I am with you always, to the very end of the age." Matthew 28:16-20**

Now you might be thinking, *"But that was ancient Bible stuff...meant for the disciples. Does it really mean that commission is for me too?"*

Yes it is for you! As you read in the last chapter, take note of how *you* are called to be His disciple. He is your good and kind Shepherd and you are His beloved sheep. He rescued you and He has wonderful plans for your life. And He is asking you to go and tell everyone about what He did for you. You must go and share your story!

You may be wrestling with feeling like this is asking a little too much, and you aren't up to the challenge. Well, I am here to tell you that you can do this. And this is where your life's purpose takes on a whole new meaning.

In fact, God can so radically encounter you that it's almost as if you've been awakened for the first time from a life of sleep. Want to hear another radical rewrite story? Okay. Then may I introduce you to Saul of Tarsus….

Saul was very good at being good. He was a big deal in his own eyes and very proud. A scholar of scholars, Saul was a super zealot who kept all the rules, and was so dedicated he ordered that Christians be killed because of old religious laws calling them "heretics." You see, Saul had never met Jesus. So one day, Jesus met Saul.

The story goes like this, Saul was on his way to Damascus when suddenly a flash of brilliant light burst all around him. It was brighter than the sun. Shielding his eyes, Acts 9 says he fell to the ground, and then a loud voice shook the ground under him. "Saul! Saul! Why are you hurting me?"

"Lord? Who are you?" Saul stammered.

"I am Jesus," said the voice, "and you are hurting Me when you hurt people who believe in Me. Go into the city now and someone there will tell you what to do." But when Saul opened his eyes, he was blind! His friends had to lead him by the hand, like a little child, into Damascus. Jesus sent a man named Ananias to visit Saul and heal him so Saul could see again. But Ananias knew of this Saul character, and didn't want to go near him. "But, Lord, he has come to hurt us!"

But the Lord assured Ananias, "Saul is the one I've chosen to tell the whole world who I am. Trust Me." So in obedience and trusting God at His word, Ananias went to Saul.

As Ananias was praying for Saul's sight to be healed, suddenly Saul could see again, but this time he saw everything differently! He even changed his name from Saul to Paul, which means "small" and "humble."

And do you know what Ananias name means? "The Lord is full of grace."

And do you know that just what Paul's message was all about from then on?

You got it.

You see, even Saul in his life of "blindness" was shown the light. If God can turn Saul's heart, he can open our eyes, melt hearts, and transform anyone.

Paul became one of the most influential apostles in the Bible, writing much of the New Testament, and was deeply involved in founding the first century Church. But he may be best known for becoming a missionary, sharing his passionate teaching on the divine mysteries of the very real relationship between the Holy Spirit and mankind. Encouraging other believers, he wrote a famous pep talk in the scriptures found in Philippians:

"I can do all things through Christ who gives me strength." Phil 4:13

Paul even experienced imprisonment, several times for stepping out in faith. And yet he rallied on the first church to become real followers of Jesus, humbly serving others and teaching on the loving and gracious character of Jesus—a new perspective! He cheered them onto higher standards, reminding them that they could do all things through Christ. Jesus, by the presence of the Holy Spirit, would give them wisdom and strength—no matter what their age, their background, their name, or their cultural upbringing.

"In the same way, let your light shine before others, that they may see your good deeds and glorify your Father in heaven." Matthew 5:16

Have you ever seen a lighthouse? In the top of a lighthouse there is a massive, bright light that is focused into a direct bean by a huge, all-surrounding lens. When it's dark or foggy on the ocean, the keeper of the lighthouse shines the beam out over the waters to help ships, guiding them into safe harbor. It's the contrast of the light in the darkness that gives it the power to lead people to safety. Jesus plainly told us that He is the light of the world. Light shows what is really there and what is true. It shows us the way.

"I am the way and the truth and the life. No one comes to the Father except through me." John 14:6

Jesus guides us with His light of truth in the midst of this world's darkness. Our radical transformations from living in His Light are just too good to keep to ourselves!

As Believers, we were made alive and we have the answer for the world. His name is Jesus! What a privilege to share His Name. What a privilege to be His ambassadors, and be used for His Kingdom purposes by *simply sharing our story.*

This is *your* season. It is a season of your dawn. You have a new name. You have taken into His Family by adoption to sonship. Your sails are filling again, He wants to carry you back into the current. It is a season of fresh hope and great purpose, positioning you for real impact in His Kingdom! So believe it! Arise and shine, for you carry Jesus, the Hope of Glory, the answer the world is desperately searching for!

You can do all things though Christ who gives you strength!

You can go and tell your story to large crowds or small ones.

You can go and intervene in someone's life who is feeling down and out by sharing your story of hope and new beginnings.

You can carry the message of His hope just by telling your story.

You can be the voice of Jesus to a dying world.

Go and share with the world that, *"Your Story Is Not Done!"*

"And I will be with you even unto the end of the earth." Matthew 28:20

Your Story Is Not Done®

Your Story Is Not Done is a campaign to amplify hope: a book and film series, it shares stories of redemption, healing and second chances when Jesus Christ, The Author of our faith takes over.

Help us spread the message and amplify hope!

Visit and subscribe for All Access
at www.YourStoryIsNotDone.com
For film release updates, blog and merch

Follow us at
facebook.com/YourStoryIsNotDone
Instagram: @YourStoryIsNotDone